The French
Art of
Living Well

The French Art of Living Well

Finding Joie de Vivre
in the Everyday World

CATHY YANDELL

ST. MARTIN'S PRESS
NEW YORK

First published in the United States by St. Martin's Press,
an imprint of St. Martin's Publishing Group

www.stmartins.com

Library of Congress Cataloging-in-Publication Data

Names: Yandell, Cathy M., author.
Title: The French art of living well : finding joie de vivre in the everyday
    world / Cathy Yandell.
Other titles: Finding joie de vivre in the everyday world
Description: First edition. | New York : St. Martin's Press, 2023. |
    Includes index.
Identifiers: LCCN 2022056771 | ISBN 9781250777980 (hardcover) |
    ISBN 9781250777997 (ebook)
Subjects: LCSH: France—Social life and customs—21st century. |
    France—In popular culture. | Yandell, Cathy M. | Americans—
    France. | Joy—France.
Classification: LCC DC33.8 .Y36 2023 | DDC 944.084—dc23/eng/20221130
LC record available at https://lccn.loc.gov/2022056771

Our books may be purchased in bulk for promotional, educational,
or business use. Please contact your local bookseller or the
Macmillan Corporate and Premium Sales Department at 1-800-221-7945,
extension 5442, or by email at MacmillanSpecialMarkets@macmillan.com.

First Edition: 2023

10 9 8 7 6 5 4 3 2 1

For Mark, Lise, and Laura

Contents

Un premier mot (A first word)   *1*

1. Celebrating the Senses   *11*

   The Joy of Cooking   18

   Making Scents   27

   Touching, Feeling   31

   Water as Healing Elixir   33

2. Shaking It Up   *45*

   In Defense of Handball and Beyond   48

   Getting Fit   50

   Dance to the Music   55

   Sex and the City (and the Country, and in Between)   57

   The French Get the Last Laugh . . . and the First   69

3. Sparking the Mind   *76*

   Savoring Books   81

   Lingering in Libraries   85

   Sleeping with Baudelaire   90

   Exploring with Montaigne   93

   Delighting in Duras   96

   Reading in Nature   98

   Seeing the Light   100

4. Finding Art Everywhere   *110*

Art Matters   113

Sculpture and Sensuality   116

Depicting Joy   121

Street Spirit   125

At the Movies   131

Long Live Music   136

5. Defining Frenchness   *141*

The Family   143

Village Life   148

Urban Neighborhoods   152

The Underdog   155

The Power of Debate   159

Public Schools   163

In Defense of the French Language   171

6. Taking Time, Making Time   *179*

Small Pleasures   182

French Life, Then and Now   184

Strolling with Ghosts   193

Taking It Slow   197

Un dernier mot (A last word)   *201*

Photo Permissions   205

Acknowledgments   207

Index   209

The French
Art of
Living Well

Un premier mot (A first word)

"*u vin, mademoiselle?*" the waiter inquired, moving the wine bottle toward my empty glass.

He had come to our long table in steerage class with a bottle of wine in one hand and a white cloth draped over his forearm to absorb the inevitable spills as the ship careened back and forth. I had never had wine before. Raised by a nondrinking Protestant family, I was hesitant.

It was decades ago, and I had come to New York from New Mexico to sail with a group of disheveled American students in the lowest possible class on one of the last crossings of the elegant ocean liner the SS *France*. The stately and dapper director of the study abroad program, a Mr. Holmes, was an American who had lived in Paris for several years. At about six-foot-five, he was a towering figure in every sense. He seemed to know everything about France, and I tried to imagine what it would be like to inhabit his body and his mind—he had so much experience with French language and culture. Plus, at his height the view must have been excellent from up there! While telling us students that we could certainly choose not to drink wine, he reminded us that wine was a point of considerable pride in France and that by refusing to try it, we would be rejecting an important element of French culture. The same was true, he said, of various French cheeses—365 of them, one for every day of the year. I liked cheese, but what to do about the wine? Dilemma.

Why have I come on this trip with over a thousand people, not one of whom have I ever met? I began to ask myself. As a child in New Mexico I had heard Spanish, Navajo, Hopi, and Zuni spoken around me, and I loved learning expressions in other languages from my friends—but I had never heard French. When I was about five years old, my mother taught me an Americanized version of the song "Frère Jacques," whose refrain "*Sonnez les matines*" ("Ring the bells for Matins," or morning prayer) became, in our pronunciation, "*Summa lumma tina.*" Later, a Belgian singer in an international choir stayed with my family, and when she asked if I knew "Frère Jacques" and suggested that we sing it in a round, I answered excitedly, "Yes! Of course!" But when she began to sing, my jaw dropped. Other than the melody, I recognized absolutely nothing about the original song. When she sang those same words, they were so different—and so beautiful. I was mesmerized. Years later, on that huge ocean liner, I reminded myself that, yes, it was all terrifying, but, yes, taking this leap was the only way to immerse myself in French.

As I sat at the table with that wine bottle poised above my glass, an image popped into my head: Walking from our spartan, submarine-style rooms to the deck, I had noticed tables of smartly dressed people speaking French, drinking espresso, and laughing, deep in discussion, as though they had all the time in the world. Well, we did have a lot of time, but how could they converse contentedly for so long? The same thought crossed my mind during the *apéritif* (before-dinner drinks) later in the day. For the French on the ship, the purpose of the voyage seemed to be the pleasure of the journey and of one another's company, while most of us Americans were ticking off the days till we landed. The French had an intriguing, relaxed insouciance about them, I thought. Something we might be missing.

My dilemma quickly dissolved, and I looked up at the waiter holding the bottle of wine: *"Oui, s'il vous plaît,"* I said.

With that first glass of wine on the ship, little did I know that I was beginning what would turn out to be a continuing journey—enjoying wine, to be sure, but more broadly, drinking in French culture, and opening up to a new world.

There is a word for it: *débarquer* (to land, to disembark). It also means "to realize," "to become aware of something." When I first arrived in Paris, those meanings coalesced.

After reaching Le Havre, taking a bumpy bus ride, and "disembarking" again into the teeming capital city, I realized that no matter what happened during the year ahead of me, monumental changes were on the horizon. The elegant women and well-dressed men all seemed so detached as they bustled by me on the sidewalk. I gazed dizzily around. How old could these impressive buildings be?

Like a stargazer who suddenly realizes she is only a speck of dust in the universe, I became all too aware of my modest stature on that Parisian sidewalk. Little wonder, as I now picture myself there: a skinny, acne-ridden teenager. To make matters worse, my short skirt, all the rage in the United States at that time, looked like a little scrap of ill-fitting material next to the longer, flowing dresses of the chic, young Parisian women. My skirt drew attention only to my toothpick legs and clunky American shoes. My long, straight blond hair in no way looked French, and every time I tried to wear a scarf, it was as though

I were either incapable of making a knot or trying to strangle myself. In short, nothing about me looked French. Clearly, I had a lot of work ahead of me.

I didn't want to become French; I wanted to *be* French—and that was a stiff order.

For the study abroad program, I had been assigned to live with the Hamels, an elderly French couple whose apartment looked onto the Champs de Mars (a field dedicated to the god of war) and the Eiffel Tower. It was magical for a small-town girl to open her bedroom shutters (another concept I had never encountered) every morning to see the sun beaming on that iconic tower and the trees below it. I would soon learn, however, that aside from the mobs of tourists passing through, the neighborhood was virtually dead—sleepy and residential. Fortunately, our classes were held in the Latin Quarter, where everything seemed more vibrant.

The Hamels were a reserved and quiet couple. The only time my assigned roommate, Diane, and I ever talked with them was over dinner. We were off to classes during the day, but early in the morning, Madame Hamel would bring our breakfast into our room on trays: *biscottes* (melba toast), apricot jam (*always* apricot), and tea. Meanwhile, people all over Paris were simultaneously feasting on freshly baked baguettes and sipping *café au lait*—but I didn't know that at the time. Nor did I know that having calf's tongue for dinner, with its spongy, bumpy texture, was not a frequent occurrence in other Parisian households. Nonetheless, I was grateful to be staying with a kind French family, delighted to hear French spoken around me, and thrilled to be living in Paris. My parents had never left the North American continent, so I was all the more aware of my good fortune.

Diane's father was the CEO of a famous (now defunct) toy

empire. When he and his wife came to visit their daughter in Paris, they generously invited me to join all of them for dinner at Maxim's, the most famous and most exclusive restaurant in Paris at the time. Both Diane and her mother wore fur. As we handed our coats over to the clerk in the *vestiaire* (cloakroom), I noticed that mine—made of dull, beige cloth with plastic buttons—was singularly the only coat in the room not made of fur. (The PETA movement, which was just then taking shape in the United States, hadn't yet reached Paris.)

Following a meal of *escargots* (snails!), *boeuf bourguignon*, and *île flottante* ("floating island," a light meringue swimming in a sea of English cream), we went to the famous cabaret spot called the Lido de Paris to watch topless dancers strut around the stage in feathers. Having been brought up in a modest family, in terms of both means and morals, I suddenly found myself in another world—puzzling, albeit intriguing. Despite my surprise, there was something about this culture I found enticing. But it wasn't the glitter, glitz, and glamour that drew me in—it was the spirit of *celebration*.

In the Hamels' apartment, I had access to the only telephone (a landline), but that brought another challenge. Although live operators had disappeared from daily life back home, France was still filled with them, and if a connection couldn't be made, the operator came on the line to see if she—it was always a *she*—could be of assistance. Each time I had to make a call, before dialing, I would stare at the phone, building up confidence and reciting the number out loud in case I was asked for it. Any number above eighty in French is a bear. For "ninety-seven," you say *quatre-vingt-dix-sept* (four-twenty-ten-seven), so if you're not quick at addition, you're out of luck. Plus, I was worried about my accent: *What if the operator knows I'm American?* (Of *course the operator will know I'm American. Dream on.*) Happily, despite my panic, the few times the operator came on, I was able to spit out the numbers more or less on cue, and she obligingly made the connection. Little by little, I warmed up to those hermetic numbers, and the telephone ultimately held the key that would unlock the door to my new friends.

The Hamels' grown children and grandchildren occasionally visited the sunny apartment on avenue de la Bourdonnais, lending a palpable sense of conviviality to those family gatherings. The Hamels' grandson Henri—a four-year-old spark plug with brown, curly hair—helped me understand exactly why the French word for "curly" is *bouclé* ("looped" or "buckled"). Indeed, all over his head were small, round loops that shook when he jumped up and down, which was frequently.

When I struck up a conversation with Henri, an immense wave of envy came over me. Here he was, *four years old*, speaking the most beautiful French in the world with no effort whatsoever, while I had been diligently studying French for those same four years, and mine was lamentable. How was that fair? The *r*'s rolled off his tongue like honey, and his high-pitched sentences were the model of linguistic purity. As the year continued, I would eventually acquire enough French to have almost any conversation about anything, anywhere. Still, even after many more years of trying, my French would never have the perfect intonation of four-year-old Henri's.

How would I ever fit in?

Patent leather ankle boots would probably do it, as nine out of ten students on the boulevard Saint Michel seemed to be wearing them. Finally, after a few months of buying virtually nothing, I gathered up my coins and my courage and walked into the Salamander shoe store in the Latin Quarter. Thanks to

Salamander (pronounced at the time with the accent on the last syllable, pronounced "-dair"), I would be as French as I could possibly be; my new French friend Eve constantly raved about those shoes. And I would get them in the year's most popular color, a reddish cordovan color, which would go well with . . . um, virtually nothing I owned. But, so what? I would look French.

The biggest hurdle was this: I didn't know my shoe size in France. If I were actually French, how could I possibly not know my own shoe size by the age of nineteen? Inconceivable! Fortunately, I learned from someone that a 36 was a size S in clothing and that shoe size often corresponded to clothing size in the metric system. So, with great fanfare (at least in my head), I waltzed into the store. When asked my *pointure*, I responded confidently, *"Trente-six."* It was working—I was making my first French purchase! I tried on the boots and walked briefly around the carpeted space.

"Elles sont jolies, non?" (They're nice, aren't they?), the saleswoman remarked.

"Oui, très," I responded, a tiny bit less confidently.

My toes were touching the front ends of the boots, but surely that wouldn't be a problem. Patent leather stretches, doesn't it? In the blink of an eye, I was shelling out francs and zipping out the door to celebrate my victory, walking down the boulevard Saint Germain with my Salamander bag for all to see. At last, I was finally going to look French.

The next morning, I slipped into the clothes that would be the least of all chromatic evils—*le moins pire* (the "least worst"), as the French jokingly say—and for the finishing touch, I donned the cordovan-colored boots. Down several flights of stairs and onto the street, down more stairs and into the subway,

I was struck by a humbling realization: My toes were not simply "touching" the ends of the shoes. They were butting against
them like the heads of opposing rugby teams when the whistle
blows. But it was impossible to go back up to the apartment
now: I would be late for class.

My full-fledged Frenchness, I'm sorry to confess, lasted only
one painful day. And by the way, as I later learned, Salamander
is a *German* company.

I did, however, make one final effort to appear French and,
by extension, to become cool. One day, I spotted a floppy brown
felt hat on a street vendor's rack that might do the trick. It
wasn't quite elegant enough to be a fedora, but it was trying
desperately to come close, and in that sense, it reminded me of
myself—not quite there, but almost. I would don the hat and
stride through Paris—past the Sorbonne, into the Jardin du
Luxembourg, and along the Seine. I would walk confidently,
and I would be miraculously transformed. This, I thought,
would be the beginning of a new life.

Every American who has set foot in France has a story—whether
you have made only a brief stopover, done a quick tourist cir-
cuit, or lived in the country for many years. Hemingway had
one, Gertrude Stein had one, and Emily, the character from the
2020s television series *Emily in Paris*, has one. Yes, French stereotypes are on display to some extent in all of them, but there
is also a grain of truth in every cliché. Despite the American
cultural baggage evident in all of these tales, we learn from
them, laugh at the characters' gaffes, relive our own experiences, and compare our own interpretations of French culture
to theirs.

The book you are now reading sets out, merrily, to celebrate and continue that tradition. But my story will not unfold over a self-revealing year in France or end happily ever after in a marriage to a Frenchman or Frenchwoman. Instead, with this book, I hope to sketch out my discovery and rediscovery, over the course of a few decades of returning often to France, of *la joie de vivre*—literally, "the joy of living." I lived in the country first as a student and later as a mother and a teacher of French literature and culture, sometimes in the context of directing a program for students abroad. While I run the risk, as the French literary critic Antoine Compagnon describes it, of exposing my own *nullité, nudité* (inanity, nakedness), I will take a few paths through culture, memory, history, and fiction to capture at least a bit of the uncapturable French art of living well.

Joie de vivre. The term evokes baguettes, berets, bicycles, Bordeaux wines, perfumes and parasols, cheeses and checkered tablecloths, elegance and ease—in short, what is *imagined* to be Frenchness. While these snapshots are certainly part of the larger picture, they seem only to scratch the surface of a culturally rooted concept. The idea of joie de vivre must be fundamentally French, if English cannot manage to come up with its own term—indeed, the word *joie de vivre* appears in Merriam-Webster's English-language dictionary.

What is it about French culture that generated the idea of joie de vivre? The first French–English dictionary, which dates to 1611, includes a few expressions involving joy: *joye de papillon* (butterfly joy), defined in seventeenth-century English as a "momentarie gladness"; and *fille de joye* (daughter of joy) as a "pleasant sinner." But there is no English equivalent for *joie de vivre*. The first use of the expression can be traced to later in that century, and then to Flaubert's novel *L'Éducation sentimentale* in the nineteenth century, but it didn't become a catchphrase until Émile Zola's ironically titled novel *La Joie de vivre* was published serially in the 1880s. (If you're looking for an uplifting read, this one may not be your best choice.) Today, the term *joie de vivre* is too often associated with rarified wine, sumptuous cuisine, and luxurious apparel, items reserved only for the white upper classes. But at all levels of class and society, the French seem to hold secrets to finding moments of joy in their daily lives.

Why is this the case? And how can we (who are not French) grasp what constitutes this *joie de vivre* that defies definition?

1

Celebrating the Senses

The first time I went to a French wedding, I had no idea what I was in for. The ceremony was held in a church, and the reception dinner in a large country house surrounded by gardens and farmland.

"Oh, so this is your first French wedding?" a few bemused guests asked me.

It started with a glass of champagne outdoors. What could be more glorious than champagne, friendly people, and an expanse of French countryside?

Once we were seated inside, in a large, open room with weathered beams, we were served an *amuse-bouche* (pre-appetizer), followed by an *entrée* (appetizer), followed by *quenelles* (fish dumplings with Nantua sauce, a specialty of Lyon, the bride's home city)—which I took to be the main course.

Topics of conversation at my table ranged from guests' places of origin to travel destinations to the current political landscape. When things had settled down a bit, and I imagined we were waiting for the wedding cake, in came a huge tray of roasted duck, *pommes sarladaises* (potatoes cooked in duck fat), and fresh vegetables. By then, I was only picking at the cornucopia on my plate and slowing down on the delicious Burgundy from a nearby vineyard. (Was anyone noticing that I could scarcely eat another bite? How many more courses could there possibly be?)

Then came a lovely salad of crisp local greens, followed by cheeses from several regions—a blue cheese from Auvergne, sheep's cheese from the Pyrenees, and the ever-creamy Saint Félicien from the Rhône Alpes—all punctuated by discussion and good cheer. At last came the *pièce montée en choux* (a wedding tower of little pastries) and more champagne, followed by coffee, followed in turn by a *digestif* or *pousse-café* (an after-dinner drink that "pushes" the coffee down). There is even such a thing as a *pousse-pousse café* (an *after*-after-dinner drink)—though I don't believe we had one that evening. And for those who could still move, there was dancing throughout the night. Though not light on my feet that evening, I did dance, but I also learned, for future reference, that wedding dinners in France are to be approached gingerly.

French culinary pride is always evident in the range and quantity of offerings, but the real point is to spend hours . . . and hours . . . engaging in conversation with people you know and people you don't know while enjoying an array of sensory delights. But this was only the tip of the iceberg in my discovery of the joy of sustained evenings. The earliest ending of any French wedding I have attended was 4 A.M., and no one over the age of ten seemed sleepy—time is subsumed by an abundance of pleasure.

Weddings are only one example of the many French celebrations focused on food. Every time I returned from an evening with friends in Paris, my French host family would ask, "What did you have to eat?" That was always the first question—which puzzled me. Not where we went, not what we saw, not what we talked about, but what we *ate*. At first, I would respond with something like "Oh, a quiche and some soup" and start to move on to another topic. But then they would want to know what *kind* of quiche and what *kind* of soup. At last, I had an epiphany: celebrations and gastronomy are inseparable in France. Whereas in the United States, we often go to dinner and then to a show, in France the dinner *is* the show. Marshall McLuhan famously declared that the medium is the message. In France, it occurred to me, the food is the message, or a big part of it—and the message is *"Enjoy!"*

Fast-forwarding several years, my husband and I, with daughters now in tow, went to my friend Josette's for Christmas dinner. At the time, our children were all in elementary school, and we were joined by a neighbor family including three children around the ages of ours. With presents in our arms for Josette's family, we arrived at the appointed hour of one-ish. to find family and neighbors all squeezed into the small apartment—there were seventeen of us, *au total*, counting grandmothers. The kitchen table, the dining table, and a folding table had all been pushed together and covered with festive tablecloths, and Josette's mother, Francine, was just bringing out her famous *œufs mimosa* to put on the table (a bit like deviled eggs, but with hard-cooked egg yolk crumbled on top, making the dish look surprisingly like mimosa blossoms).

Francine is from Perpignan, speaks with a strong southern accent, and has the biggest heart one can imagine. Chauvinistic regionals claim that everyone from Perpignan is open and welcoming. I haven't yet met enough residents of the city to confirm this stereotype, but it is certainly true of Francine. Jean-François, Josette's charming, jovial brother, who is rotund, with a ruddy face and smiling eyes, opened the champagne without the usual loud pop, like a pro. He belongs to a wine club, and other than the professionals, he knows more about wine than anyone I know—and he finds secret good deals and suppliers at every turn. He is happy to explain the *terroir* and soil quality necessary for the champagne or wine in question, the percentage of each type of grape involved, and which years the climatic conditions were ideal for winemaking. While he doesn't go so far as to describe the "hints of leather with a blackberry finish" you often see on California wine labels, he has an expert's palate. That day, he had brought not only champagne, but also some delicious Côte de Nuits, a prized Burgundy, for the main course. I will not be able to reconstruct all the courses, but the pièce de résistance was roasted *chevreuil*.

What is a chevreuil? I thought, not really wanting to know.

The creature we were about to eat was presented on a tray propped up on its front legs, as though in Cobra pose. Everyone clapped as the platter was carried in from the kitchen.

Hmm, I thought. The word began like *cheval* (horse), but the dish looked too small to be that. *How do I finesse this? I don't want to be the squeamish American.*

Chevreuil turned out to be "deer" or "venison." I thought back to the time a hunter friend brought some venison to my family long ago, and we found it perfectly palatable. Venison is considered a delicacy in France, and we Americans were apparently the only ones to find those front legs in the least troubling.

Jean-François carved the *chevreuil* and, with plates passed to him, served everyone as we gave our preferences: "*Un tout petit peu, s'il te plaît*" (just a little, please), for my part.

I've forgotten to mention that, during this time, the bright green partridge, the neighbors' pet, was flying all around the room, much to the delight of the children, who tried to get it to perch on their fingers or land on the table next to them. As you can imagine, though, there was virtually no space on the table. The French keep their pieces of baguette next to their plates as they eat, and the partridge had figured this out quite easily, landing and pecking crumbs from time to time in the little space that was left.

Meanwhile, our daughters were trying to remember all the verses to "A Partridge in a Pear Tree," and the seven children present had all joined in singing the verses in both French and English. The song turned out not to be easily translatable, however: In French, the final line is *"Un moineau tout en haut du pommier"* (A sparrow atop the apple tree). And our very favorite part, "five golden rings," is *"cinq gros poussins"* (five fat baby chickens)—not quite the same vibe!

The children were allowed a tiny glass of wine mixed with water—to be held with "panda hands," palms flat against the stem so they wouldn't drop it. At one point, they got up to play games in the bedroom while the adults stretched a bit on the balcony—and still the meal continued, very slowly, throughout the afternoon and into the evening.

At around 8 P.M., out came the awaited *bûche de Noël* (Christmas log), this one from a local bakery. It is a magnificent creation of cake rolled into the shape of a log, containing as much chocolate as it can hold, as well as layers of cream filling. For the most elaborate versions, shaved chocolate is added for the "bark" as well as realistic-looking mushrooms made from meringue. Sumptuous.

The enjoyment continued with coffee and a *digestif.*

Between 11 P.M. and midnight, we thought we'd gather up the children, thank our hosts and friends, and be off—but no.

Frédéric, the father of the three neighbor children and a prized Vietnamese-born chef, suddenly declared, *"La soupe à l'oignon!"*

Ah yes, something we hadn't known: the Christmas dinner in this family must be topped off with an onion soup at midnight. So we continued, exchanging ideas and stories until, after helping to clean up as much as Francine would allow, we at last began the slow walk home to our apartment on the avenue des Gobelins.

I cannot recall how late we slept the next day, but fortunately, our calendar was clear. Celebration, cooking, friendship, laughter, and the delight of intergenerational company completed our first dream-worthy Christmas in Paris.

These grand celebrations are not isolated phenomena in France. They're simply a macro example of micro events that happen every day—a dinner with friends, a lunch with colleagues, a coffee on a boulevard, a picnic in a park.

I was at first shocked to learn that Article R4228–19 of the French Code du travail (Labor Code) specifies that it is illegal to eat at one's desk or "any premises designated for work." After much public grousing during the pandemic, a temporary exception to the law was passed in the National Assembly, with an emphasis on "temporary." Eating at work would never be permanently allowed, of course.

Why these draconian measures? Food in the workplace can be a bother—as you know if one of your colleagues has ever brought in stir-fry with fish sauce and left it sitting on the counter in the break room all afternoon. But more important, lunch is meant to provide a moment away from files, business meetings, building construction, and garbage collection. It is meant to be a break from it all, for all, a moment to enjoy—rather like a momentary vacation (which we Americans have a hard time taking). Going to a café, restaurant, brasserie, or bistro gets you out of the office, shop, or factory. And as the French say, *ça vous change les idées* (it gets your head in a different place). There may be a cafeteria in the workplace, but even then, it's a respite that happens not at your desk or work station, but elsewhere. And even if people are in a hurry to return to work, there's always time to fit in *un petit café*, an expressed black elixir that punctuates the meal, simultaneously signaling the end of this reprieve and the beginning of renewed energy for the afternoon.

And as if the pride in French gastronomy were not sufficiently pronounced on earth, it has now conquered outer space as well. While American astronauts' meals have typically included peanut butter, macaroni and cheese, and applesauce, the French astronaut Thomas Pesquet hoped for better cuisine on his 2021 flight on the SpaceX rocket. Alain Ducasse, arguably the most celebrated French chef today, was approached about making some space-ready meals, which he happily agreed to do for all the astronauts on that mission. During their orbits, they enjoyed beef bourguignon, potato cakes with wild mushrooms, and almond tarts with caramelized pears. But some adjustments had to be made. There is a no-tolerance alcohol policy in space, which presented quite a challenge for the beef bourguignon, which is always made with red wine—but Ducasse found a solution: He prepared the slow-cooked beef and vegetables with wine, but then extracted the alcohol through a spinning evaporator that kept the flavor intact. A nuclear magnetic resonance instrument was then used to confirm the absence of alcohol in the dish. The sauce also had to be made a little thicker than usual to keep the droplets from floating away in zero gravity.

Despite Ducasse's team's great success in producing mouth-watering meals for the astronauts, the attempt to make croissants that would hold up in outer space failed disastrously. You can be transported to the heavens with pleasure, but to consume some French delicacies, it would seem, you have to keep your feet firmly on the ground.

THE JOY OF COOKING

Eating French food and cooking it are of course two different matters, and my first official experiment in cooking was calamitous. When I returned to France during graduate school, I was living in an apartment by myself in a big city for the first time. I needed only a very small space, somewhere to "squat" while I did a year's worth of research at the National Library and finished writing my dissertation. On the rue de Caumartin, which was then a prime red-light district, I found a tiny studio with a thin divider allegedly forming a kitchen and a bedroom. The makeshift kitchen consisted of a burner; a mini refrigerator; a small, weathered table; and two metal chairs. The "bedroom" had two twin beds smashed against each wall, with enough room between them to allow only the thinnest person to pass. The room was dark with one small window about waist high. But I was in Paris on my own!

One of my first outings was to an outdoor market to get ingredients for the first fully French meal I would cook. I knew how to make *tostadas compuestas* and green chile stew with Hatch peppers from my native New Mexico, but now I was going to be a real French cook! Coming from the desert, I was particularly looking forward to cooking fish, which was a frugal but still very French choice.

The fish in the market were displayed whole on piles of

ice. I chose a shiny grey bream, which the fishmonger carefully wrapped in white butcher paper. Then I tucked the package into my newly purchased *filet* (string bag), wended my way among the friendly sex workers who had begun to recognize me as a neighbor, and climbed the narrow, winding stairway to my third-floor digs. When I unwrapped the fish in my apartment and saw its eyes staring up at me, it seemed to be asking why I had taken its life away. I burst into tears.

So began my first attempt at cooking an authentic French meal. Many years and several cooking courses later, my favorite dish to make is the French classic *saumon à l'oseille* (salmon with sorrel sauce), no eyes included. However, that initial encounter made me more aware of the fish-person connection and nudged me in the direction of vegetarianism.

For many French people, *vegetarian* simply means you don't eat beef. The confusion probably originates in the word *viande*, which means "meat" but often stands in for "beef," as in *viande hachée* (ground beef). Several of my American vegetarian students have encountered host families who have said, in essence, "Oh, you don't eat meat? No problem—we'll prepare chicken!" Although in recent years, finding families to host vegetarians has become much easier; when faced with a vegan, a French host will commonly respond, incredulous, "But you don't even eat eggs and cheese?"—both staples in the French diet. "What *do* you eat?"

While vegetarian and vegan restaurants have sprouted up throughout France, there remains some resistance to the trend. In response to the campaign "Save the Planet—Eat Vegan" from a few years ago, a counter-slogan emerged: "Save the Farmer— Eat a Vegan." But vegan foodies in France have pushed back in style with gourmet offerings. Le Potager de Charlotte (Charlotte's

Vegetable Garden) in Paris serves asparagus risotto with pine nuts, chestnut soy yogurt with candied pecans, and cashew cream with goji berries. And this kind of fare can be found not only in Paris, Lyon, and Marseille, but also in smaller towns like Arras (at Mezzaluna, which specializes in organic Mediterranean dishes). Les Petites Graines in Saint Étienne serves lentil cakes with butternut mousse, and rosemary-infused figs and oranges for dessert. Le Resto du Village in rural Normandy takes pride in its mushroom and chestnut "steak" on a bed of garlicky spinach and in its calvados (an apple brandy) and caramel apples with almond cream for dessert. Even confirmed carnivores may find resistance futile in this inventively delicious cuisine.

The love of food has permeated almost every aspect of French culture, including its language—sometimes with dangerous results. President Emmanuel Macron, confident in his ability to speak fluent English, had these words for Australia's then–prime minister Malcolm Turnbull at the beginning of a formal speech in Sydney: "Thank you and your delicious wife for your warm welcome and the perfect organization of this trip." Needless to say, that exquisite gaffe became front-page material for the international English-speaking press. *Ah, those Frenchmen . . . !* But, for the French, *délicieux* is a catchall word, meaning "wonderful," "terrific," "cool," and "awesome," but evoking the sensuality associated with savoring scrumptious delicacies. I recently overheard two middle-aged Frenchmen discussing their looks, with one of them proudly declaring, *"Je suis délicieusement vintage"* (I am deliciously vintage). Somehow, I couldn't imagine that sentence being spoken by an American man, but I was intrigued by the framing of one's advanced age as a sensually enticing state.

A host of French idiomatic expressions are based on food:

Avoir la pêche (to have the peach) means "to be full of energy."

Occupe-toi de tes oignons (literally, take care of your onions) means "Mind your own business."

Raconter des salades (literally, to tell salads) translates as "to spin yarns."

Mettre de l'eau dans son vin (to put water in one's wine) means "to tone it down" or "to compromise."

En faire tout un fromage/plat (to make a whole cheese/dish out of it) means "to make a big deal of it."

Mettre du beurre dans les épinards (to put butter on the spinach) means "to earn some extra money."

C'est la fin des haricots (that's the last of the beans) means "That's the end of the line."

The word *savoureux* (tasty) functions in much the same way as *délicieux*. A sign in a bookstore wished all of us *de savoureuses lectures* (tasty readings) for the summer. In a book review, I recently read about a *roman délectable* (a delectable novel)—so good you could eat it. In that same vein, *alléchant* (tantalizing, enticing), often used to describe books, plays, and television series, comes from the verb *lécher* (to lick), suggesting that many sensations can be more fully interpreted through the pleasures of taste. It is obvious from these expressions that, whether explicitly or implicitly, very rarely is cooking or food completely absent from the mind of a French speaker.

A few years after my disastrous first French cooking experiment, my friend Mary and I invited our graduate professor to dinner. With his bluest of eyes and in his angelic voice—no, neither of us was trying to get with him; as everyone knew, he was gay, another loss for straight women—he had made the French Renaissance come alive for both of us as he read Joachim du Bellay poems for the class. An accomplished gourmet cook, our prof had prepared a chef-worthy meal for his seminar the year before, with a luscious cold avocado soup and . . . I don't remember what else, but it was all stupendous.

The day of our dinner arrived and, with Julia Child and the Troisgros brothers advising me via their cookbooks, I was ready. Mary would make the appetizers and the dessert, and I would prepare the main course, a salmon soufflé, which had turned out beautifully the week before when I tested it—I was not taking any risks. The evening began with olives, perfect little canapés with caramelized onions and goat cheese prepared by Mary, and a Sancerre wine we had scrupulously chosen with what little wine savvy we possessed.

I preheated the oven to 400 degrees Fahrenheit and, at the appointed time, inserted the soufflé dish into it, turning the temperature down slightly as instructed. Forty minutes later— the timing was perfect—I went into the kitchen to retrieve my prize. But when I took the soufflé out of the oven, although it was warm, it was also as flat and as wet as it had been when I put it in.

"Oh, no problem," our patient guest said. "Just cook it a bit longer."

Fifteen minutes passed . . . with the same result.

What could I have done wrong? I thought. *I'm certain I beat the egg whites into soft peaks and folded them in.*

Back to the oven the soufflé went, for another ten minutes.

Finally, our professor blurted out, "Oh, I'm sure it'll be fine. Let's just eat it!"

As I took out the soufflé for the last time, and we began to eat the gluey substance—which my professor and Mary both claimed to be delicious in spite of its texture—it at last dawned on me: I had left the lid on the dish the whole time! Something about oxygen and egg whites . . .

French cooking would forever remain slightly out of my reach.

There are many unspoken rules regarding dining and invitations in France. Unfortunately, I had to learn them one at a time, each lesson embarrassing in its own way. The first thing I remember learning is that eight o'clock (the most common French dinnertime) does not mean eight o'clock. In fact, if you ring your host's doorbell at precisely 8 P.M., he will probably take a minute to answer the door, and when he does, he will likely have a towel hastily tied around his waist, with water dripping all over the parquet floor. In short, eight o'clock means 8:15 at the earliest, the *quart d'heure parisien* (the Parisian fifteen minutes of delay)—which is even longer in the South of France. I've been told that the *quart d'heure toulousian* (the quarter hour of delay in Toulouse) is half an hour.

After experiencing a dripping host, the next time I was invited to dinner by someone, I arrived fashionably "on time," between 8:15 and 8:30, with a bottle of Bordeaux.

That should do it, I figured.

But then the host said, "Un Bordeaux, merci! We tend to like Bourgogne for red wine, but that's okay. We're having filet of sole tonight anyway, so we'll be drinking white."

Another miss. But, no problem. Live and learn, right?

The next time I was invited for dinner, everything was set: I arrived after the appointed hour, and I brought flowers. Now I was really on a roll. The door opened, and I was greeted with a smile, but a little less than warmly when I handed the mother of the family some carefully arranged red-and-white carnations from the little flower stand on the corner.

"They're lovely," she blurted out, stammering only a little.

Understanding that I'd somehow committed a grave error without knowing exactly what it was, I asked, "I'm sorry. Are you allergic?"

"Not at all," she replied, as the rest of the family came into the room, all eyes turned on me. "It's just that . . . carnations are generally for funerals . . . a sign of death." (And, as I've since learned, the same holds for chrysanthemums.)

I sincerely apologized, and fortunately, we didn't dwell on the subject too long, but in the back of my head all evening I heard dirges in a minor key, drowning out any hopes I might have had for traversing the Grand Canyon of our cultural divide.

Some cultural divides in France, however, have become bridges. The colonial legacy looms large in France, not only in the French imagination, but also in French cuisine. So many influences from immigrants who settled in France have been woven into French culture that it is sometimes impossible to separate them out. A Parisian friend recently assured me, with no hint of irony, that couscous is a fully French dish. It is true that a grain similar to semolina is mentioned as *coscosson* in Rabelais's epic tale *Gargantua*, written almost five hundred years ago. But the dish the French now call couscous—complemented with vegetables, chicken, beef, or *merguez* (spicy sausage)—is indisputably North African in origin and became popular in France only after the two waves of immigration by Algerians, Moroccans, and Tunisians following World War II and at the conclusion of the Algerian War of Independence in 1962.

Even the quintessentially French croissant comes from the Islamic crescent symbol—but with Austrian origins. In 1683, during the Siege of Vienna by Turkish forces, according to a popular version of the story, Austrian bakers, who worked largely underground, alerted the army when they heard the Turks digging a tunnel into the city to take it over. To celebrate the Austrian victory, the bakers made bread in the shape of crescents (from the Turkish flag). While legend claims that the Vienna-born Marie-Antoinette first brought croissants to France, records indicate that it was the Austrian baker August Zang who opened the first Viennese bakery in Paris, in 1838. But that's only part of the story: the buttery, puffed, multi-layer delicacy we know today was later developed in France and was declared a French national product in 1920.

What about the most French of all French breads, the iconic baguette? Each year, France holds a baguette-baking contest, Le Grand Prix de la baguette, judged blindly by a group of chefs and other dignitaries. The winner has the privilege of supplying the Palais de l'Élysée (presidential palace) with bread for the following year. For four of the past six years, much to the amazement of staunch traditionalists, the winners of the contest have been from families who emigrated from Africa—three from Tunisia and one from Senegal. Entries are judged on *la cuisson* (the baking), *l'aspect* (the appearance), *l'odeur* (the aroma), *le goût* (the taste), and *la mie* (the "crumb," or interior).

One of the winners of Le Grand Prix de la baguette, Mahmoud M'seddi, describes the key to a perfect baguette: passion. "You could have exactly the same recipe," he said, "and if one person is more passionate than the other, they'll have a better result. Even if you've done exactly the same thing, it won't be the same. It's like magic." According to M'seddi, it's also important for the baker to *feel* French. "Whoever wins the contest is someone who's passionate about French culture, who has become integrated as a French person," he added. "We need to make people proud to be French."

Indeed, that seems to be one of the mottos for the whole of French cuisine: to make people proud to be French. (The other is to invite them to enjoy.)

Mory Sacko's restaurant in the Parisian *quartier* of Montparnasse gives us a clue as to where French cuisine might be headed. The child of Malian immigrants, Sacko left school and worked in several prestigious restaurants in Paris, including the Mandarin Oriental, before opening his own restaurant in 2020. Its name, MoSuke, is a combination of his first name and the only known samurai of African origin, Yasuke. Raised in France, Sacko became enamored of Japan from watching anime as a child, and his extensive knowledge of Malian cooking originated in his mother's kitchen. For his restaurant, he invented a cooking style that creatively combines aspects of the three cultures.

Restaurant MoSuke soon gained a star in the *Michelin Guide*, one of the fastest ascensions for any restaurant in history. A few months later, Sacko was invited to host a new cooking show, *Cuisine ouverte* (Open Kitchen), in which he cooks alongside a different celebrated French chef each week, adapting French classics to his own eclectic style. Before each cooking experiment, he interviews the various people responsible for each fresh ingredient—a cultivator of olives from Marseille, a tomato farmer from Provence . . . To date, the show has garnered more than a million and a half viewers.

What does the future look like for this sort of culinary fusion in France? In short, if you're looking for a table at MoSuke, plan your dinner at least several months in advance!

MAKING SCENTS

What do Opium, La Petite Robe Noire (The Little Black Dress), Séductrice (Seductress), L'Interdit (Forbidden), Scandal, and Libre (Free) have in common? They are all among the bestselling perfumes for women in France. And for men? Homme (Man), Sauvage (Savage), L'Homme Idéal (The Ideal Man), Mâle (Male), and Légende. The fragrances for women evoke intriguing but contradictory images: gendered stereotypes (little black dress, seductress), norm breaking (Opium, Forbidden, Scandal), or freedom from it all (Free). With the men's fragrances, a man can be wild, ideal, or legendary, but he remains fundamentally male. Maybe these names are meant to reassure alpha males that they, too, can wear perfume, but the essentialist associations are telling, reminding us that the images a particular perfume conjures up are at least as important as its fragrance.

Historically, perfume originated before the advent of deodorant, to conceal body odor. But Catherine de Médicis (the spelling she used in France), queen consort, regent of France, and influential adviser to three kings from 1547 to 1589, has been credited with making perfume fashionable. Renato Bianco (known in France as René Bianchi), imported along with Catherine from Italy, became the queen's perfumer (and, for conspiracy theorists, her poison maker). Thanks to his work, Catherine reportedly distributed perfumed gloves to her entourage. Her letters do not suggest to me someone obsessed with fashion—have you seen her later-in-life portrait? Instead, in Catherine's letters, you see her strategic quest to promote the Valois dynasty, but no musings on the scents of the day. Still, it makes for a good origin story.

Tucked away on a hillside above the Côte d'Azur just north of Cannes, in the Alpes-Maritimes, lies "the perfume capital of the world," Grasse, population fifty thousand. Its historic center remains a beautiful medieval town, with cobblestone paths, red-tile roofs, and a Romanesque church. Grasse boasts the International Perfume Museum and seventy-some perfume companies, including the famous houses of Fragonard, Galimard, and Molinard. Much like wine tasting, perfume analysis has a vocabulary all its own: As a student of scent, you learn about the top notes, heart notes, and base notes of each fragrance. You immediately understand why so many flowers flourish here—thanks to Grasse's microclimate and its elevation of a thousand feet, and with temperatures ranging from 41 to 82 degrees Fahrenheit throughout the year, the flowers that make up the industry's perfumes bask in the Mediterranean sun but never wilt with heat. Blankets of lush lavender, violets, lilies, jasmine, mimosa, and roses ripple over the hillsides. Breezes permitting, your senses will carry you to imagined paradises: jasmine-scented hammams in Istanbul, romantic English rose gardens, peony-surrounded Japanese temples. Originally, all perfumes were made from the distillation or maceration of flowers into essential oils, which were then crafted into fragrances. Although many scents are chemically produced today, when in Grasse, I can think only of breathing in flowers as I look out over the fields, my senses overtaken by olfactive pleasure and visual beauty.

Colorful and scented flowers—except for carnations and chrysanthemums!—are an excellent gift when you are invited over for dinner in France. Fortunately, in large cities, several flower shops dot the streets of almost every neighborhood, with buckets of colorful and fragrant jonquils, daisies, rhododendron, tulips, and lilies, depending on the season. One August day, when all of Paris seemed closed, I found online that only one flower shop was open in my neighborhood. With not much time to spare, I pushed open the door to the tiny boutique Muscari, on the boulevard du Port Royal, and peered in. A scruffy, *café-au-lait*–colored dog with a wildly wagging tail came toward me and popped out its head. I hesitated, wondering if the dog was permitted out on this extremely busy street.

"Il peut sortir, sans problème" (He can go out, no problem), a voice from inside shouted.

So, I entered—but the dog followed me back in, wagging his tail like a salsa dancer and brushing up against the big buckets of flowers. He then ran over to a cage with a parakeet sitting on top of it and began looking up at the bird, prancing and barking all the while.

I was not prepared for the potpourri of sensory treats within the shop, and I hardly knew where to walk among the buckets of dahlias and roses and peonies. On one wall hung a baroque-looking gold clock that, not surprisingly, was a few hours off. From among the buckets of flowers, on both the floor and tables, emerged the occasional colorful pinwheel or blue cobalt vase, a child's wooden table with chairs, or neo-classical Greek busts with flowers growing out of them. And squeezed between buckets on the left side of the boutique, next to a marble fireplace, stood a life-size silver stag with large antlers.

"What kind of bouquet would you like?" the owner asked me in French as she straddled one of the buckets. Meanwhile, the parakeet began to fly around the room just past me, and the dog tried to follow it, wagging his tail and running into several objects and me on the way.

"Um, what do you suggest?" I asked, dizzily trying to take it all in.

The owner told me her name. Was it Aurélie? (She could not have been friendlier.) Her skin-tight bronze-colored pants would have fit impeccably had it not been for the ripped seam on one side, letting a few inches of flesh creep through. Aurélie noted that she and I were among the only Parisians left in town on this August day. I asked if she herself would soon take a vacation, and she said yes, but only after the coming weekend, when she would be supplying the flowers for a wedding with three hundred guests.

On a back wall was a whiteboard with names of flowers scribbled on it. How did she make sense of it all, and navigate her way around these motley buckets, and dog, and parakeet, and stag, and all the other paraphernalia I haven't mentioned?

"Do you like these dahlias?" she inquired. "What about a few fern stalks as well? What colors shall we use? Shall we make it a *bouquet sauvage*?" she asked, referring to a wilder-looking bunch. By now I had completely forgotten the time, reveling as I was in these scents of freesia and roses and in the discussion with Aurélie.

Just as she was tying the twine around my now-formed bouquet, the parakeet took off again, and the dog headed after it in excited pursuit, knocking over only one brass statue on the way.

"He has caught her only about three times," Aurélie explained, "but I've always been able to intervene."

I wondered how she could possibly concentrate in all the madness, but she seemed quite happy—and accompanied by my beautiful and divine-smelling *bouquet sauvage*, so was I.

I would be late for dinner, but, well, did it really matter?

It turns out that, for the French, scents are crucial, and not only in floral arrangements but also in cars. Only in France . . . Imagine pulling up to an Auchan gas station and seeing a sign for three products: AIR, ASPIRATEUR, PARFUM. One euro will give you five minutes of access to air for your tires, a vacuum, and a perfume dispenser for your car. It isn't clear which perfume is in the dispenser at any given moment, but you can also buy scented air fresheners: lemon, jasmine-sandalwood, sea breeze, and caramel-vanilla. (Maybe not!)

"Un bonheur qui ne dure pas, on appelle ça du plaisir" (A happiness that doesn't last, we call that pleasure), says Madame de La Pommeraye in *Lady J*, a film inspired by Diderot's *Jacques le fataliste*. What could be at once more pleasurable and more fleeting than a waft of coffee, roasting chestnuts, or flowers? Nuanced scents can be ethereal, transporting you to a world beyond this one. Granted, car perfume is a different story.

TOUCHING, FEELING

The first time a French friend grabbed my arm and tucked hers under mine as we walked down the street, I had two quick thoughts: First: *Will someone get the wrong impression?* And second: *This is a warm and welcome way to walk, especially when it's cool outside.*

If you've been to France, you have probably seen people of all ages walking arm in arm and kissing each other on both cheeks (*faire la bise*) as a greeting. Lovers kiss on bridges, in the métro, and on park benches without the slightest hesitation. For the French, what's known as one's *bulle personnelle* (personal bubble) is quite small compared with that of some outsiders. It's not unusual for Americans to back up when a French person begins to speak to them face-to-face, or to recoil when not knowing which people they should kiss or which cheek to kiss first. And how many kisses?

To confuse things further, the answer to that question is "It depends." It's two kisses in Paris, often three in parts of the South of France, and in some northern places, even four. I cannot count the number of times I completely blew the exercise when it was new to me: bumping noses when I didn't know which side to go for first (the answer is usually right cheek to right cheek first, but if you're standing with the left cheek more available, that can be kissed first), slobbering on a guy's cheek ("It's not a *real* kiss, dummy! It's an air kiss"), missing the connection between cheeks entirely, or even causing a head-on collision. Men are often spared the expectation of the *bise* among other men, substituting a handshake or *un check* (a fist bump) for a kiss.

Whatever the style, the fact remains that physical contact, however conventional, is central to daily life in France. Following the long Covid-19 pandemic, during which citizens were urged never to *faire la bise*, one might have imagined that the custom would be slow to return, but the greeting is such an integral part of French life that it sprang back in many circles with the rapidity of a bow releasing its arrow.

A study cited in Gaël Brulé's *Petites mythologies du bonheur français* (Brief Myths on French Happiness) ranks France first among seventy-seven countries in *hédonisme*, defined as "pleasure" or "sensuousness" as manifested in physical closeness (holding hands, kissing, having sex), eating, drinking, and smoking. This ranking points not to a measure of composite happiness, but rather to an

archipelago of little pleasures that make up daily life. This international reputation has a long history: the first Italian guidebook
to France, published in the late seventeenth century, described it
as "the country of desire."

The multipurpose words *doux* (sweet, soft, puffy, slow, gentle, quiet) and *touche* (touch) speak volumes about the presence
of "touching" in spoken language. A shampoo labeled as *ultra-
doux* will leave your hair soft to the touch. *Doux* wines will
be sweet to drink with your *douce* (sweetheart). Your *doudoune*
(down jacket) will keep you warm, and a child's *doudou* (blankie)
will make him feel safe. Pet the cat *doucement* (gently) and speak
doucement (slowly, quietly). The sound of someone's voice can be
doux (sweet, mellifluous). The word *touche* similarly appears in
multiple contexts: *toucher son salaire* means "to get paid"; *touche-
touche* signifies "bumper-to-bumper"; *sortie de touche* indicates
when a ball is "out of bounds." All these expressions connote
touching or being touched—and reinforce the notion that sensuality is omnipresent in everyday French language and, by extension, in daily French life.

WATER AS HEALING ELIXIR

Humanity is naturally drawn to water, but the French seem to
celebrate it more prominently than many other cultures, most
visibly in their fountains. François I's palace, with its Renaissance construction dating from 1528, bears the name Fontainebleau. Historians have proposed various hypotheses about the
origins of the name, but one possibility is an evolution of "Fontaine Belle Eau" (Fountain of Beautiful Water). Fountains can
be found in virtually every town, and Paris has hundreds of

them (not that they work all the time). The fifty-some fountains of the Château de Versailles (Louis XIV's gilded palace not far from Paris) are heralded each summer with the Grandes Eaux, a celebration of the fountains with music and light. Water, water everywhere—a balm for the spirit. Even drinking fountains have been multiplying in France of late. To discourage the purchase of water in plastic bottles, more than a dozen *fontaines pétillantes* (fountains of carbonated water) have been installed in Parisian parks, and many more are being planned.

Water has always been prized as a source of daily pleasure in France, as evidenced by the still-visible Gallo-Roman baths on the corner of the boulevards Saint Michel and Saint Germain in Paris. These thermal baths served as a center of conviviality for Lutetia (the city's name in Latin) beginning in about the third century. The Thermes de Cluny, arranged in heated and cooler rooms much like spas today, are thought to have been active for only a few centuries. They are now part of an archeological site in and around the Musée de Cluny (the National Museum of the Middle Ages), in the Latin Quarter.

Fast-forwarding to the Renaissance—pilgrimages were made to thermal baths throughout France in this period, for healing or recreation. In Marguerite de Navarre's *Heptameron* (inspired by Boccaccio's *Decameron*), water also plays a central role. Whereas in the Italian text, storytellers are holed up in a country house to avoid the plague, in the French text, a flood strands Marguerite's storytellers on their way home from the thermal baths in Cauterets (which remains a spa town today) at a monastery on the river Gave. There, they settle onto a meadow near the river each day and tell tales as a pleasant pastime while the bridge is being repaired. Today, Marguerite and other French queens are represented in a semicircle of statues above the central fountain in Paris's Jardin du Luxembourg, as if to associate royal sumptuousness with water.

Thermal baths at hot springs have had historical and contemporary success in Germany and Italy, but the birth of *thalassothérapie* (thalassotherapy, or seawater therapy) took place in France, where both the Atlantic and the Mediterranean coastlines are now dotted with pristine spas for healing and recreation. Medical spas using seawater for rheumatism and depression were constructed on the northern Atlantic coast of France as early as 1800. From the outset, seawater therapy was meant to address both mental and physical ailments. The practice did not fully take off until the 1960s, when the three-time victor of the Tour de France, Louison Bobet, who was injured in a car accident, used seawater treatments to rebuild his stamina. Bobet and his brother subsequently contributed to the popularity of the treatments, which today can be enjoyed at more than fifty establishments in France.

My friends Jean-Louis and Eve (a different Eve from the one I mention in the preface, "Un premier mot"), both medical practitioners, engage in at least a week of thalassotherapy together each year for relaxation and rejuvenation. Jean-Louis says that one of the strengths of the process is that the water provides a womb-like environment, enveloping the body like a cocoon. With thalassotherapy, you undergo a kind of regression, where you are invited to "let go," but where you can also regroup and *reprendre des forces* (recharge).

When I first heard of these doctor-prescribed *cures* (treatments) of three weeks in a thermal spa, I was incredulous. *You mean the French can spend three weeks in a spa covered by national health insurance?* The answer is yes, but it's a little more complicated than that. First, if your hydrotherapy is to be *conventionnée* (covered by insurance), your doctor or specialist must prescribe it by filling out a nationalized form during the trimester that precedes your chosen spa dates. Your rates of reimbursement will be higher if you get a recommendation from your primary physician before seeing a specialist. How do you become eligible to get a spa vacation? (They don't call it that.) First, without fail, you must have one of the following conditions: arthritis, rheumatism, osteoporosis, lower back pain, sciatica, fibromyalgia, hemorrhoids, varicose veins, thrombosis, phlebitis, asthma, bronchitis, prostatitis, intestinal problems, slow metabolism, high blood pressure, vaginal dryness, hay fever or other allergies, acne, scars, or muscle stiffness. (Who hasn't had stiff muscles?) In other words, everyone qualifies!

The amount reimbursed by national health insurance depends on your financial situation, but the government covers at least 70 percent of the treatment costs for all those with a prescription. For those below a certain income level or with a severe illness, the national health insurance covers 100 percent of the cost of the treatment, including transportation and lodging. Regardless of the nature or the severity of your condition, the course of treatment prescribed must adhere to the following regimen: eighteen days—the figure of eighteen must have been arrived at by some Cartesian formula—six days per week (with no treatments on Sundays), for three consecutive weeks. You may have had the same thought I did: Couldn't you do the treatment in three different stages if you're not free for three consecutive weeks? You could, but then the treatment would not be *conventionné*. No exceptions.

I have always been intrigued by these vacations—I mean *cures*—that so many French people seem to take advantage of, and I really wanted to try one myself. Of course, not being a

French citizen, I do not qualify for the underwriting of such a treatment. And even if I were a French citizen, it turns out that not *everyone* qualifies after all—it depends on the severity or the recurrence of the condition. I consulted my friends in the field of medicine to find out the best (preferably honest) means of entry, so that I might at least see some of the treatments from the inside. They made clear that the overall program of treatments (for medical purposes, including meetings with doctors) is not the same as thalassotherapy (for preventive health, comfort, and well-being, with no doctors involved), but that many of the treatments are identical.

With this close parallel in mind, I signed up for three days of thalassotherapy (as distinguished from the required three weeks for a thermal *cure*). Taking a train to Royan, on the Atlantic coast of the Charente-Maritime, about three hours from Paris, I arrived at the hotel, one devoted exclusively to thalassotherapy. There I was greeted warmly at the check-in desk by Florent, a trim young man with cropped brown hair. He told me I had been *surclassée* (upgraded) to a room with a sea view, presumably because those rooms had not filled during the aftermath of the coronavirus pandemic. The room, however, was not quite ready. While waiting, I walked around the seaside town, taking in its typical square, white two-story houses, its winding lanes, its port filled with sailboats, and its views of the Atlantic from the tops of hills.

When I returned to the hotel later, the dapper Florent was no longer at the desk, so I addressed the woman who had replaced him. At first, I couldn't think of the word, so I said that I had been *élevée* (raised), and we both smiled, she bemusedly, and I with tail tucked under me, as it dawned on both of us—*Ah, oui! Surclassée!*—what I meant. (For a split second, she must have wondered how exactly it was that I had been "raised." As a child? From the dead?)

When I arrived in the thalassotherapy center the next morning, I felt as though I had come to my first day of kindergarten. The woman at the reception desk gave me a list of *soins* (treatments), but I didn't know what the names meant. "Enveloping in remineralizing algae" seemed fairly self-explanatory, but what, exactly, was the "hydromassaging bath"? Or the "pediluve" ("foot," as in pedestrian, and "luve," as in antediluvian)? And the most intriguing of all, the "thalaxion" (Action by seawater? What action?).

My first *soin* was the "remineralizing algae." Manon, a beautiful woman whose parents were from Morocco, called my name. At least, I *guessed* she was beautiful—we were wearing masks, as some pandemic restrictions were still in place, but her eyes exuded both warmth and depth. I asked her which treatment she most liked to administer, and she replied without hesitation: the *modelage sous fine pluie marine* (massage under light ocean rain). Now beginning to like everything that Manon recommended, I decided to sign up for one for the next day.

The small algae room contains only a table about the size of a bathtub with what looks to be an air mattress on it. Manon gave me the choice of leaving my swimsuit on or removing it. The algae would have been either all over my swimsuit or all over my skin, so I easily opted for the latter. She slathered the thick green substance all over my back, stomach, legs, and arms and then wrapped me in a kind of film (like cling wrap) that she assured me was biodegradable.

"You're not claustrophobic, are you?" she inquired in French.

"No," I assured her, as I began to get a tiny bit apprehensive. *Isn't this supposed to be relaxing?*

She then turned on some calming New Age music and left the room, closing the door behind her.

The suspense was palpable. The warm mattress I was lying on began undulating under my feet like an ocean current, and then, little by little, it closed in on my entire body (except for my head, thank goodness), while continuing to undulate. The current flowed slowly from my feet to my shoulders—it was like being on a warm waterbed, with someone else making the waves and guiding them. About twenty lovely minutes went by like this. Eventually, both the music and the movement of the mattress stopped, and Manon came back in to tell me that I could now get up and wash off all the greenery in the shower.

"There are great benefits to having algae with sea minerals on the skin," she announced.

"What benefits?" I asked.

"With the warmth of the mattress and the wrap," she assured me, "some of the minerals can penetrate the skin—they are relaxing and good for the muscles."

If she says so! Still, it had felt surprisingly wondrous to be rolling around in that green cocoon.

Next came the *douche au jet* (jet shower), which I had imagined would be a kind of Jacuzzi with multiple jets. I now saw how wrong I had been. Picture a bare tiled room equipped only with a stool and a firefighter's hose on one side and a metal railing on the other. It reminded me of the tiny interrogation room I had been in long ago for five hours on the Czech border when my companion tried to enter the country with a blacklisted book in his suitcase—which, granted, was not such a good idea at the time.

But, back to the *douche au jet*!

At that moment, a sadistically smiling woman entered the

room, took a seat on the stool, and began questioning me in French:

"Have you ever had this procedure before?"

"No, it's my first time."

"Your very first time?" Her smile grew a bit wider and her eyes more intense. "Hold on to the rail," she shouted as she turned on the roaring hose. The pummeling "jet" was indeed like a fire hose . . . or a geyser . . . or a tsunami. First, the attendant motioned for me to stand in profile as she aimed the stream above my shoulder blades, almost knocking me over. Then she directed it at one side, pushing the stream up and down from shoulder to ankle.

When facing away from her, I could feel the stream attacking my shoulders, blasting down one side of my spine, and then rotating around the buttock on each side from the center outward, in a circular, clockwise motion on the right, reversed on the left. The only truly painful part was on my tight quads in the front, up and down, up and down.

The woman with this instrument of torture assured me that the deep beating would relax my muscles and get rid of cellulite. My only thought was that if my muscles survived the ordeal intact, I would consider it a modest success.

Manon had been right. Of all the treatments, my favorite was the "massage under light ocean rain," where the hydrotherapist exerted pressure on my back as warm "rain" fell, allowing my body to release and relax. And during this light "rain," I at last understood: the water both enhances and extends the treatment. Imagine the taste of a wine that lingers in your mouth long after you've swallowed it. Professional wine tasters count that lingering sensation in "caudalies," or seconds of discernable flavor. Similarly, the warm rain flowing down my body extended the effect of the strokes down my arms, back, and legs. The sensations continued and continued for many caudalies.

After all these treatments, my eyelids became heavy, my muscles released, and the weightiness of the body—the connection between body and earth—felt reassuring rather than debilitating. My breathing was slower, fuller. At last, I was grasping how these kinds of treatments—especially when funded by the French government—can be restorative for both body and psyche. Three days of this regime seemed just right for my American sense of time, but I could imagine that, after three weeks, I would have either merged permanently with the earth or been bouncing off the walls. I'm not sure which.

Outside the hotel, all along the rocky path above the shoreline, outdoor exercise equipment was available for everyone, and I made use of it on the sunniest days. But even bad weather could be exhilarating here, as I experienced while running along the beach in Royan, near the hotel, with the rain beating down on me and the wind blowing at my back. I had become an exuberant sailboat . . . and also a fan of this particularly French method of curing ills.

Heavenly Hammams

Water therapy in France is not, however, limited to the ocean or to hot springs. I have been several times to the hammam (Turkish bath) at the central mosque in Paris with my friends Yasmina and Malika. Our religious backgrounds make for a rather odd trio at the mosque: Malika is a practicing Muslim; Yasmina's father was raised in the traditional Amazigh (Berber) religion, and her mother is a nonpracticing Catholic; and I was brought

up with what might be called Heinz 57 Protestantism, a motley mixture of Protestant influences. Religious conflict exists in
France, of course—but personal relations are a different matter.

The first time I stepped into a hammam—the name is de-
rived from the Arabic word *hamma*, meaning "to heat"—I was
welcomed into a world of warmth and magic. After checking
our belongings at the *vestiaire* and receiving towels, an exfoliating loofah mitt, and some black soap (made from Castile soap,
olive oil, macerated olives, and wood ash), we proceeded into
the hot steam room—not for the faint of heart! When you've
stayed inside it almost long enough to pass out, you can then go
into the Moroccan-tiled room with the vaulted ceiling and the
many water spigots. First, you put black soap all over your body
and allow it to soften the skin for about ten minutes. Then, using the buckets provided, you pour hot water over your head all
at once, like a powerful waterfall.

Because Malika was a specialist in back scrubbing (and
happy to teach us her trade), we did not need to reserve the
services of a professional to scrub us with the exfoliating mitts.
Those women are notoriously strong and do not hesitate to press
down on your skin, scrubbing it until it begins to flake off and,
occasionally, even drawing blood. (Yes, that has happened to me.)
But Malika's touch was firm without being harsh. I wish I could
reconstruct in my memory exactly how she held Yasmina and
me, one by one, as she scrubbed our torsos and backs with the exfoliating mitt. She pushed us gently into her weight-bearing arm,
encouraging us to let go of all tension and fall into a reassuring
and powerful embrace. All sensation floated upward and dissi-
pated into the steam. Those moments may be as close to an ideal
afterlife as I will ever get. And I may even have written a bad
poem about the experience, inventively titled "In Malika's Arms."

On another day, Yasmina, Malika, and I set out for a different hammam, in the north of Paris, and decided to stop for a coffee at an outdoor café on the way. As we sat at the table, we noticed that cars driving by were slowing down and sometimes stopping so that the driver and riders could stare at us. When we finally realized what was happening, we began to laugh till we cried. We must have been a bizarre sight: Malika, an olive-skinned, hijab-wearing Muslim woman whose body was covered from head to toe; Yasmina, a beautiful, voluptuous dark-skinned woman in a low-cut blouse and skinny jeans; and me, a plain-looking, broom-colored blonde.

Whatever brought them together? the gawkers' stares telegraphed.

The answer was no different from what usually brings three people together in a Parisian café, whatever their backgrounds—friendship.

Later, when we walked into the hammam, it was as if the outside world had paused. The pristine pool lined with turquoise and blue Moroccan-style Zellige tiles called to us, but first we had several stages of scrubbing, heating, and steaming to enjoy. When at last we reached the cool-water pool, we did slow laps before entering the tearoom, where the scent of mint transported us to a lingering oasis of peace.

I have now been to several "hammams" in different cultures. In a Japanese public bath in Osaka, I was stared at as though I were an alien. At a small hammam in the medina (the original walled-in area of North African cities) of Rabat, the native Moroccans greeted my friend and me like long-lost relatives. The most opulent hammam I have ever seen was also the most bereft of life: the beautiful marble pools had never been used. The hammam was located in the lower level of the Hassan II Mosque in Casablanca, the only mosque tourists are allowed to visit in all of Morocco. Built for show, the mosque has a Disneyesque quality. It is immense and stunningly gorgeous, with a gleaming white minaret searing the sky as the waves of the Atlantic crash at its foundation. Although it was constructed to hold seven thousand worshippers, only a handful of locals were present in the mosque on the day my students and I visited.

The traditional mosque's function is much like that of an ancient cathedral: erected at the very center of a town or village, it served to unite the townspeople and satisfy their spiritual and social needs. But this mosque was missing the closeness and communion that, even as a non-Muslim, I had felt elsewhere—in a mud-walled prayer room in Bamako, Mali, and in the Mohammad Al-Amin Mosque, in the central square of Beirut. But the hammam at the central mosque in Paris, replete with its not-always-working fountains, will always be my favorite.

Hammams were originally included in mosques so that Muslim men could perform their ablutions before praying, but they also serve as gathering places for men and women. If a hammam is not large enough to allow for a segregation of the sexes, then it is usually kept open on different days for men and women. (There have been no nonbinary days as yet.) Currently reserved for women, the hammam of the Grand Mosque of Paris provides a haven of warmth where bodies of all colors, shapes, and sizes happily congregate and commune.

2

Shaking It Up

The French clearly savor the pleasures of the physical: engaging in sports, sex, and laughter. To begin with the most important, anyone who has spent more than a few hours in France knows that soccer is not merely a pastime in L'Hexagone (France's nickname, based on its shape). It is the sport to end all sports, the game that stops both clocks and traffic. A recent newspaper headline read, "Because Not *Everything* in Life Is Soccer . . ." During the world championship games, if all goes well for "Les Bleus" (the French national team), soccer unites the entire country, which speaks with one boisterous voice. The famous expression *"Black, blanc, beur"* (Black, white, Arab) was first coined to describe the victorious French team of the 1998 World Cup, which included Black, white, and North African–origin players. The term *Black*, pronounced with a French accent, was the cool designation for Black Frenchmen at the time, and the term *beur*, still in use, comes from *verlan*, a form of French slang. *"Black, blanc, beur"*—a play on the *bleu, blanc, rouge* (blue, white, red) of the French flag—seemed to describe a new France, a welcome conglomeration of French natives and immigrants, all living together in harmony on the soccer field, as in French daily life. And that image couldn't be more accurate . . . for ninety minutes at a time. During those ninety minutes, any internecine disagreements among ethnic groups vanish like steam rising from a tiny cup of espresso.

Even though the World Cup championship game of 2018 was to take place in the afternoon, we arose early to stake out a spot for viewing it on a big screen in Paris. You could of course watch the game on your own television (and for those who stayed home, shouts could be heard in unison throughout the courtyards of the city), but unless you were fortunate enough to travel to Russia for the finals, the real way to be a part of it all was to go to a café or bar where the game would be projected. There you could share the experience with as many people as could possibly be crammed into the space, all cheering loudly. An indignant *"Hors jeu!"* (Offside!) would resound through the crowds, *"Ouaaah!"* (Yessssssss!) would erupt for a corner kick, and *"Allez, les Bleus!"* (Go, Blues!) would be chanted in unison, which would eventually bring about the desired point. At that moment, all of France would be there together on the field, not far from the goal, hurling the white orb past the goalie and into the net.

All over Paris, excitement was in the air. French flags of different sizes hung from a thousand windows, appeared on bicycle handlebars, sprouted from hats and goggles. Heavily tattooed teenagers, otherwise disengaged and chain-smoking, now sported French flags around their shoulders. Even the most jaded, least patriotic types had them. With arms flailing and legs kicking in their strollers, toddlers wore the blue, white, and red jerseys of the French team.

My husband and I wanted to join in a neighborhood gathering, so we headed for the Place Edgar Quinet near the Montparnasse Tower. Even though the game wouldn't begin for hours, things were already hopping. A kind waiter offered us the very last two seats with a view of the big screen in Pizzeria Pinocchio, and even though we hadn't planned to have pizza for lunch, we jumped at the occasion.

The two young women sharing our table were from Marseille and showing their provincially laced joy to be in Paris for the festivities. Already jubilant, they downed tall glasses of Stella Artois at an impressive rate. Truth be told, they had initially come to Paris for the Beyoncé concert, but when they learned that France would be in the finals of the World Cup, they exchanged their train tickets for a later return.

Tallish and lanky in that oh so French way, both Hélène and Juliette were dressed with exquisite simplicity: skinny jeans with white *baskets* (sneakers) and variations on a flowing, thin peasant blouse, their long hair pulled back into not-quite-ponytails. After a few exchanged stories, we were the best of friends, Parisians at heart who simply loved, *loved* Les Bleus. For the next few hours, everyone in the café was joined together in the battle along with the French team, as if the outcome of the Franco-Prussian war rested on our shoulders.

When the timer sounded at ninety-five minutes with a final score of 4 to 2 for France over Croatia, complete and total elation broke out in Place Edgar Quinet. Lampposts were scaled by athletic young men, one of whom was gleefully mooning the crowd, to the bemused gazes of passers-by. Others climbed on top of bus stop shelters and jumped up and down. Firecrackers could be heard throughout Paris. Drivers rolled down their windows, shouting the final score, with pedestrians gleefully echoing them. We boarded the métro to go to the Champs Élysées, the epicenter of French celebrations, our collective weight nearly exceeding the limits of what the subway car could hold. As our fellow riders jumped up and down, the car shook as if the train would careen off the track:

"On a gagné, on a gagné!" (We won!) resounded from station to station.

A picture-perfect couple dressed in African *boubous* (flowing, wide-sleeved robes) and brightly flowered shirts stood in the middle of the car; their baby was wearing a tricolor headband with a big bow. Everyone seemed to be smiling at the perplexed baby, as if to say, "We just won the World Cup, and this ebony French baby wearing the team's colors is beyond adorable."

It was the kind of moment that the Franco-Czech writer Milan Kundera calls "kitsch," a moment infused with a self-indulgent sentimentalism, but I swear that all of us in that métro car were in it together, drinking up the last drop of the World Cup.

IN DEFENSE OF HANDBALL AND BEYOND

For years, I'd heard my French friends jubilating over France's World Championship titles in handball, and I admit that I couldn't muster up much enthusiasm. I was touched by their elation, but I considered the French victory in handball a bit like being absolutely the best triangle player in an orchestra. I pictured racquetball without a racquet, a game where players throw a ball against a wall, ensuring that it bounces no more than two times before the next player hits it—a sport sometimes called wallball in the United States. It's aerobic and no doubt amusing for the players, but what's in it for the spectators?

It turns out that, all that time, I had the wrong sport in mind. That is, just as "football" in the rest of the world is what Americans call soccer, so "handball" isn't what Americans call handball. On that subject, didn't George Bernard Shaw say something about the British and the Americans being separated by a common language? My family and I couldn't stop laughing when we saw a sign in an English parking lot: NO FOOTBALL COACHES (meaning "No soccer buses"). We were picturing burly, nimble-footed men being turned away: *Rugby coaches are fine, but definitely no football coaches!* Similarly, French motorists in the United Kingdom crack up at the warning sign on the motorway SOFT VERGES (meaning the road's shoulders)—*verge* in French refers to the male sexual organ.

But back to the matter at handball!

Handball dates back at least to the ancient Greeks. Homer mentions some version of it in *The Odyssey*, but the game as we know it today became popular in Europe in the nineteenth century. The sport appears to the uneducated viewer—that would be me—as a cross between basketball and soccer. It is played on a court with soccer-like goals, and a goal is scored when the ball passes between the goalposts and fully over the line. The five players on each team (plus goalie) may hit, push, or catch the ball with their hands, arms, or knees, but the ball must not touch them below the knee.

Handball is the third most popular team sport in France after soccer and basketball, as measured by the number of members in sports clubs around the country. In my experience, however, the sport far outweighs basketball, probably because of France's renown in it. Ever since the handball World Championships were inaugurated in 1938, the French men's team has taken first place more than any other country (six wins), while the women have had two wins, and both teams took gold in handball in the 2021 Olympics in Japan.

Another interesting phenomenon on the French sports land-scape is the rise of women in sports in general, notably soccer. A few of my American students joined a women's soccer team in Issy-les-Moulineaux, just southwest of Paris, and I asked them how they liked being on the team.

"Very much" was the reply.

"How do they compare to your team in the States?" I asked.

A few seconds of silence ensued.

"Are they not as strong technically?" I ventured.

"Oh yes, very talented, skillful," they replied, though I could tell they were holding something back.

"So, what's the problem?"

"Nothing, really. It's just that they're not as . . . aggressive. They love playing the sport, and they're good at it, but they don't go for the kill—and they don't experience the thrill of winning." Ah.

The following year, however, the French team made it to the quarterfinals of the Women's World Championships in soccer. The times for women's sports in France, they are a-changin', and the women are reaping the joys of their success.

GETTING FIT

A grandiose movement toward *l'urbanisme sportif* (sports-minded urban planning) and the democratization of sports is taking place in France, and the postpandemic liberation seems not to be the only reason for it. A high tide of bicycles, scooters, *gyro-roues* (self-balancing unicycles), skateboards, joggers, and roller skaters can now be seen in public spaces, which have become open-air gyms. Parkour, the urban sport of running, jumping, and turning on obstacles like walls and ledges, is also popular in France. Indeed, the name "parkour" comes from the French *parcours* (the way through, the path). One French website with a very French name, street-work-out.com, lists public exercise spaces in sixty parks within Paris's city limits. And the trend has reached far beyond the capital: Boussières-sur-Sambre, a pastoral village of 530 habitants near the Belgian border, recently installed an outdoor public exercise station that has been packed every day. The beach town of Six-Fours-les-Plages, near Marseille, has three exercise stations with ocean views. In some centers, the outdoor equipment has rivaled that of nearby gyms, with hydraulically adjustable cylinders, touch screens, and free coaching apps. Soon there will reputedly be big screens with complete workouts.

I am excited by the idea that the French government has provided so many public spaces for exercise and sports. When compared with expensive gym memberships in the United States to which not everyone has access, these free parks really do open the fitness phenomenon to anyone who would like to be a part of it.

Walking in the 14th arrondissement one day, at the end of rue Didot, I stumbled upon a small park with an area designated for *la musculation de rue* (street bodybuilding). Midafternoon on a weekday, it is not surprising to see virtually no one here. However, a five-year-old *maghrébine* (of North African origin) girl named Lola was trying out different activities. Her mother was helping her reach the handles of the elliptical trainer and the rings of the gymnastics equipment. My favorite piece of equipment was a seat with big handles that, when pulled down, lifted the chair, but Lola couldn't activate them on her own. She and I alternated on the rowing machine, with her mother helping her push the handles hard enough to get the "boat" going—all three of us laughing and chatting in the shady, quiet park, relishing the respite, knowing that the end of the workday would soon bring to a close our quiet haven as the after-work crowds poured in.

On a breezy July afternoon in the section of the Jardin du Luxembourg that extends toward Port Royal, I spotted three pairs of men engaged in boxing matches. Upon closer observation, it seemed to be a class, or maybe a practice, with the more experienced practitioners coaching the less experienced ones. Prancing, jumping, ducking, lunging, the men threw punches energetically but stopped just short of their opponents' faces. Their loose T-shirts and shorts hung from their bodies, dancing in the wind. It struck me that formless clothing was rare in this fashion-driven city, but they wore it well.

Meanwhile, a plethora of other activities unfolded around me, and I was impressed by the ethnic *mélange*. Looking down the *allée*, I saw some white adolescent girls who seemed to be new to the *espace fitness* (fitness area). One hoisted herself onto the parallel bars and began circling her legs, as if riding a bicycle. (An original use, but why not?) A trim Asian man in sweats began doing endless pull-ups while his white friend joined in, completing only about five of them. The friend, whose face was red with effort, lost his grip on the bar, fell to the ground, and landed clumsily on his feet. A frizzy-haired, olive-skinned youth with skinny arms tenuously approached the high bar, his two female companions observing with bemused interest. Ten pull-ups seemed to be a nice, round number, for show. A young white couple arrived in stylish gym clothes and began to lay out their various ropes and equipment. No kidding, the Asian athlete was still doing pull-ups. (How many? Two hundred?) Meanwhile, a Black man arrived and began jumping rope, while a white woman hung from the high bar, bringing her knees to her chest for abdominal strength. Past them, another Black man in a white T-shirt, blue shorts, and high-top sneakers practiced his hip-hop moves to the sound of a giant boom box. Back on the high bar, an Arab man did pull-ups with a weighty backpack.

It was exhilarating to see the varied faces of France gathered there that day.

The "Jardin des Voltiges" in the Parc de La Villette, in the north of Paris, is the largest *espace fitness* in France. It is unique in having been designed, in collaboration with a few city officials, by those who would use the space: bodybuilders and *traceurs* ("tracers," the nickname for those who do parkour). I set out to see it (and maybe do a few push-ups myself), only to find that, when I asked the guards at the edge of the Parc de La Villette where it was, even they didn't know anything about it. No signs or maps in the area indicated its existence.

After much circling around, I finally arrived at the park, glad to see that it was being well used. A sign calling for ETHICAL ETIQUETTE was posted at the entrance, inviting visitors to respect themselves, others, and the equipment and to be *solidaires* (an oft-used word, meaning in this context "We're all in this together"). There were three major "zones": the first for workout, weight lifting, and cross-training, the second for general fitness and what they call "ninja" (coordination), and the third for parkour. Without exception, all the participants on this day were male athletes of color.

The pavement looked like asphalt, but it is in fact made of

a springy composite material specially designed to cushion hard landings. Despite the rule prohibiting children in the space, several children stormed the area and clambered onto the exercise equipment without really using it, laughing and frolicking about—the forbidden (and too big) fruit.

Finally, I wandered over to the parkour area. For me, this was the most fascinating part of the park, though obviously the most challenging—on this particular day, no one was there. A sequence of *boules d'équilibre* (balance balls) looked both impossible and tempting: Three black balls about two feet in diameter were suspended from ropes on either side. The challenge was to climb on a foam perch and then jump onto the first ball and then run from ball to ball as fast as possible without falling. Bear in mind that not only do the suspended balls move as you step on them, but they also rotate! I quickly realized that this particular challenge was light-years beyond my balancing capacity.

Ahead, from near the ground all the way up a wall, were what at first looked to be hand grips but were actually foot grips. In parkour, as you run the course, you can push off the wall, and the foot grips will allow you to go higher and higher. I tried these with gusto and found myself getting a bit addicted to the idea—you could work your way up higher on the wall, little by little . . . Not that I made it beyond the first level, but it did seem like a good method for progressing.

All these *espaces fitness* are funded at least in part by the Agence nationale du sport, which distributes government and private subsidies for physical activities and sports throughout France. In 2021, the agency announced that it had ramped up its activities with a view toward the 2024 Olympics in Paris—which doesn't make immediate sense, given that those who are training for the Olympics are probably not the ones who might drop by a local park for a few pull-ups. Still, by 2024, everyone in Paris is to have access to free exercise space and equipment within five minutes of their home. However tenuous the connection between the Olympics and the exercise mania in France may be, it's all for a good cause!

DANCE TO THE MUSIC

Depending on what moves you or draws you in—whether at a large venue like the Palais Garnier in Paris, or the Opéra national de Lyon for ballet, or scores of smaller theaters featuring contemporary dance and other dance forms—France is filled with opportunities both to dance and to watch others dance. Countless clubs, bars, and outdoor dancing spaces invite everyone of every ethnicity, age, and sexual orientation to dance.

Before coming to France, I had taken contemporary dance classes in New Mexico, and one of the first things I wanted to do when I arrived in Paris was to find a place where I could continue to dance. The multicultural nature of the city immediately became part of my life when I began studying under a Caribbean-born dancer who described herself as being from the West Indies. She taught her classes in both French and English, addressing French students in French and international students in English.

I had hoped for a class exclusively in French, but Anna Mittelholzer, who studied with Martha Graham and performed with Pina Bausch, couldn't be beat. I loved the way Anna said, "Aaahms up!" in what seemed to me at the time to be a British accent. Her French was also so good that I first thought she must be a native speaker. I wanted to sound like her and, especially, to dance like her, but of course, neither of those desires was realistic. But what a privilege to study with her in France!

Anyone who loves to dance will be well served in Paris. You name it, it's there. Over the years, I have dabbled in modern, contemporary, Afro-Caribbean, Japanese *butō*, ballet, floor barre, North African belly dance, swing, hip-hop, and salsa—none of them with great finesse, but all of them with enthusiasm and pleasure. At the Centre de danse du Marais, you can find classes seven days a week, well into the evening. If you'd like to practice your moves in a less formal setting, you can join others in the open space at the 104 (aka Cent-quatre), on the banks of the Seine, or on the esplanade of the National Library.

For those who like to stay up all night, you can dance in one of the famous or not-so-famous clubs, to the beat of famous DJs, electronic dance music, or live music, from roughly midnight to 6 A.M. Guards at the door size up the customers to decide who may enter the hallowed space. My students give the following advice to newcomers who would like to be admitted upon their first attempt: Dress well and wear black. And if you identify as male, unless it's a bar for gay men, bring women.

Spontaneous dances are often the most fun, but some places are known for their recurring pop-up dances, notably the *bal populaire* (informal dance) Rock et Musette, in the Jardin Tino Rossi, on the Seine, every Saturday and Sunday afternoon from 2 to 6 P.M. Most of the participants there are older, dancing swing and slow dances, but they are energetic and dexterous, and anyone who so desires can join in. In the evenings at the same location, tango rules until midnight.

Dance to the music!

SEX AND THE CITY (AND THE COUNTRY, AND IN BETWEEN)

Ne reprenez, Dames, si j'ai aimé
Si j'ai senti mille torches brûlantes . . .

(Do not reproach me, Ladies, if I have loved
If I have felt a thousand burning torches . . .)

Louise Labé (1524–66)

In soft focus, the camera zooms in on a woman's shoulder covered by long sable curls, pans past her waist, and settles on her exposed thigh. The light is golden and filtered. Then, only these words can be heard, spoken in a breathy, deep tone: "Carte Noire. *Le café du désir.*" (Carte Noire. The coffee of desire.) Cut to a cup of espresso.

The fact that a tiny cup of coffee has no logical connection to a woman's thigh—the coffee might be spilled on it?—or to her sexual desirability seems not to concern anyone. The aesthetic beauty of the ad seduces coffee drinkers into buying their own very French brand. (Never mind that Carte Noire was bought by the Italian company Lavazza in 2016.) A brief generalization might be this: whereas American advertising attempts largely to inform and persuade, French advertising almost inevitably aims for seduction.

Frenchness and seduction have long been linked in the public imagination, from Queen Margot's multiple lovers in the Renaissance to Proust's cattleya (a sexually charged flower that stands in for making love in his *In Search of Lost Time*) to the real-life sexy actors François Civil and Hafsia Herzi. Indeed, being seductive has become so much a part of French national identity that it is sometimes assumed to be a fait accompli. A young Frenchman recently told me, exuberantly, "Of course American women will love me. I'm F*rrrr*ench," he purred, using the most guttural *r* imaginable.

This sexual confidence is not, however, universally shared. The pressure to be attractive to the opposite sex dominates French sites on the internet: "How to seduce a woman" and "How to be a great lover." (Answer: "It's less about technique than about alchemy between two or more people for whom pleasure is the key.") While the French blogosphere has been traditionally dominated by heterosexual seduction, now the gay community is also having its time in the spotlight. Yet, in the public imagination, binary divisions still prevail. As men and women try to conform to the gendered stereotypes of French sexual prowess, they are also confronted with their own inadequacies: "What if I can't live up to the model of the French stud/sex goddess?" But because of, or maybe despite, these "great expectations," sex is never far from the collective French consciousness. Androgynous or cross-dressing pop stars such as the talented singer-songwriter-dancer-choreographer first known as "Christine and the Queens" (as of late 2022, known as "Redcar") and Bilal Hassani (a cross-dressing singer-songwriter who represented France in the Eurovision competition in 2019) illustrate the pushback against established masculine and feminine ideals, but their sexy dance moves show that a rejection of stereotypes does not equal a rejection of sex.

In the 1990s, my friend Agnès, a young woman from Pau, in southern France, came to stay with our family in Minnesota for a few months. One day, when Agnès came home from window shopping downtown, she asked me, "Am I not attractive to American men?"

"Whatever are you talking about?" I replied. "Of course you're attractive."

"Well, I was just wondering," she continued. "Because men don't stare at me at all here—they glance at me and then they avert their gaze."

Ah, yes. I told her that American men have been taught not to stare. It's considered impolite, and it could seem as though they were stalking their prey.

"Why?" she asked, incredulously. "What could be the harm in looking?" To Agnès, if she dressed well and looked good, why shouldn't men be allowed to look at her?

And then there's the other side of the coin. When I direct a program for American students in France, some of the women tell me they feel uncomfortable when Frenchmen stare at them in the streets of Paris or on the métro. Worse, they complain, men occasionally even approach them and make suggestive comments.

Harassers do exist, to be sure, but they are not ubiquitous. And whatever cultural differences there are concerning male-female relations in France, though sometimes difficult to navigate, they are not unbridgeable. If all goes well, as it usually does, American women eventually learn that not all Frenchmen are lechers, and Frenchwomen learn that American men are probably not as disinterested as they may first appear.

While Agnès did not acquire a boyfriend during her stay in Minnesota, she did receive a clumsy invitation from a young man to "come up to my dorm room and drink champagne." She gracefully declined.

✿

In France, the subject of sex is also omnipresent on the airwaves and in the press. France Culture, the most prestigious and intellectual radio station in France, lists its most popular programs at the top of its website. And what was the number one replay during the pandemic lockdown? "Sex Toys and Liberation." And the most intellectual of newspapers, *Le Monde*, includes a weekly column on sex (sometimes worthy of the front page) called "Le Sexe selon Maïa," in which the pseudonymous writer Maïa Mazaurette enlightens her readers on all things sexual.

It turns out that, in tune with the times, sex toys have fully entered the ecological era. Recyclable and rechargeable sex toys can be purchased at Praline et Priape (as in Priapus, the Roman god of fertility, often depicted with full erection). Maïa proposes (tongue-in-cheek . . . or elsewhere) that should you find it too much trouble to return these products for recycling, you could always use them for doorstops or as dog toys. And you can buy condoms and organic lubricating cream free of parabens, alcohol, coloring, or perfume from an auspiciously named French company, the Green Condom Club.

In one of her recent columns, Maïa counseled unsuspecting readers—whether they were single, married, LGBTQ+, straight, of age or not—to imagine a sexual utopia: "What would your ideal sexual encounter look like? With one person or several? In a chalet or while watching the Bosphorus flow? Would there be talk or not? Would there be 'preliminaries,' penetration, or neither? In fact, would you really even like to have sex?" Somehow, I can't imagine such a column appearing in *The New York Times* (or *The Wall Street Journal*). How about in *USA Today*? On Fox News?

Another of Maïa's columns includes a contemporary *Carte du Tendre* (a topographical map of love) for those over fifty. The original seventeenth-century *Carte du Tendre* was an excellent example of sentimental cartography, a map in the shape of a uterus, replete with continents, islands, and seas. The geographical sites on the map—named "Inclination," "Respect," "Dangerous Seas," "Submission," "Eagerness," "Goodness," "Negligence," "Indifference," and "Tenderness"—are all to be navigated in the game of love.

In Maïa's contemporary version, predictably, a protruding "peninsula" is named "Nineteen-Year-Old Paradise." Other names include "Communication," "The Menopausal Route," "The Andropausal Route," and "The Archipelago of Fantasies." Something for everyone!

The question of sex enters into French cultural life in yet another unusual way. Do you know what happens if you fail to make eye contact with someone while clinking glasses during a toast in France? You guessed it: not just bad luck, but *seven years of bad sex*. Drinking etiquette is a serious business, clearly—but sex even more so.

Sexuality is fully a part of the French public sphere, including in politics, and seemingly with fewer hang-ups than in Anglo-Saxon cultures. Although the combination of sex and politics is not unique to France, French history overflows with "dangerous liaisons" and scandals. In the early 1300s, the French king Philippe IV's daughters-in-law infamously had adulterous affairs with Norman knights in the "Tour de Nesle affair." The Renaissance king Henri II preferred his mistress, Diane de Poitiers, to his wife, Catherine de Médicis, to such an extent

LA MER DANGEREVSE

Terres

Reconnoissance R.

Tendre sur R.

Constante amitié

Obeissance

Tendresse

Tendre

Sensibilité

MER

D'INIMITIÉ

Grands Services

Empressement

Assiduité

Meschanceté

Petits Soins

Medisance

Soumission

Perfidie

Complaisance

Indiscretion

Orgueil

Nouuelle

Tendre sur E.

Bonté

Respect.

Exactitude

Generosité

Probité

Grand Cœur

Sincerité

Billet doux

Billet galant

olis Vers

Inesgalité

esprit

Negligence

LAC
D'INDIFERENCE

Oubli

Legereté

Tiedeur

F.C.

| 2 | 4 | 6 | 8 | 10 |
Lieues d'amitié

that he built for Diane the most beautifully situated château, Chenonceau, which sits above the river Cher. He also had a goblet fashioned in the shape of Diane's breast. The story has been called apocryphal, but it was recounted in several contemporaneous sources and endures in oral history even today. To add to the Valois dynasty's salacious reputation, rumors circulated that Henri's daughter Marguerite de Valois (sometimes called Marguerite de France) had as a lover a certain Joseph Boniface de la Môle, who was executed for conspiring to kill the king Charles IX. Protestant pamphlets claimed that she had embalmed and preserved his severed head. Meanwhile, her brother Henri III kept himself surrounded by male minions and never produced an heir. Louis XIV's sex-filled reign has been sensationalized in the Franco-Canadian television series *Versailles*, but historians have confirmed that much of it is indeed reflected in records of the time.

In 1899, French president Félix Faure died in the drawing room of the Élysée Palace with his mistress (according to one version of the story) or his "psychological adviser" (according to another), who was regularly sneaked into the palace through a secret entrance. The most widely repeated reports claimed that Faure died in the arms of his half-naked mistress Marguerite Steinheil. Opposition newspapers had a heyday following the news of Faure's demise: the literary periodical *Gil Blas* reported that he died in "an excess of good health," and *Le Journal du peuple* opined that he had "sacrificed too much to Venus." French even has a term for dying during orgasm—*l'épectase*, a word curiously (or maybe not so curiously) lacking in the English lexicon.

French president François Mitterrand and his lover of many years had a daughter who reached adulthood with his personal and financial support before the news was released to the public, which posed no problem for Mitterrand's political legacy—in contrast to the media explosions following U.S. president Jimmy Carter's mere admission of "lust in his heart." (The two presidents were contemporaries.) In contrast, Mitterrand has been widely praised, both for his accomplishments as president and for keeping his private matters both responsible and private.

In 2014, tabloids featured French president François Hollande in a famous escapade of traveling incognito across Paris on a scooter to see his then-secret lover (now partner). For the record, she was neither the mother of his four children nor the woman who had accompanied him on the campaign trail and with whom he shared an apartment. Hollande was furious— not because his infidelity had been exposed, but because he considered the publishing of any information about his sex life an invasion of privacy. Indeed, whereas in Great Britain or the United States, reporters would have hounded the president and his associates to get a scoop, the scandal died down as quickly as it arose—which is not to say no political cartoons were drawn depicting it!

Sometimes, though, even in France, sex gets in the way of a favorable public opinion. Benjamin Griveaux, a candidate for the mayoral elections of Paris in 2022, entered into a virtual relationship with a twenty-nine-year-old woman in which he texted her sexually explicit videos of himself. Her live-in partner, a Russian, confiscated the videos and published them as part of a series meant to unmask politicians' hypocrisy. Online comments on several websites following an account of the story demonstrate the varying reactions of the French public:

"He has betrayed his family. He's not fit to be the mayor."

"What does Griveaux's sex life have to do with his fitness for the job?"

"A little naïve, isn't it, Benjamin, to fall into such a silly trap? The rest is a private matter."

"When you're a candidate for mayor, you can't film yourself in sexual positions that might be leaked to the public!"

"When your penis is in the place of your brain, it's the Russians' fault."

Sex and politics make for strange bedfellows, both in France and elsewhere. But even though *discrétion* is the byword among the French for the mixing of sex and politics, sex never seems to be completely obscured from the public consciousness.

Popular television shows often tell us more about the pulse of a culture than official studies, and the contemporary French television series *Plan coeur* is no exception. Its title—sometimes referred to as *Plan cul* ("Booty Plan," "One-Night Stand," or "A Friend with Benefits"), *The Hookup Plan*, the show's title in English, gives us a direct entrée into the show's focus. The series features a character named Elsa, whose morose obsession with her ex prompts her friends to set her up with a male escort (without her knowledge) so that she feels confident enough to begin to date again. One day, the hired escort waits for Elsa outside her workplace, in front of the picturesque Hôtel de Ville (City Hall). He introduces himself with the improbable name of "Jules Dupont" (the French name for "John Doe"), and the project seems to work like a charm. The friends' plan backfires, however, when sparks between the two fly, common interests are discovered, and Elsa and Julio (his real name) begin to fall in love. Disaster awaits.

Episodes with such titles as "The Party Plan," "The Lame Plan," The War Plan," and "The High and Dry Plan" introduce so many adventures and unexpected developments that I will not attempt to recount them here; nor will I provide spoilers. But besides a slight stalling of the plot in the second season, the three-season series takes viewers on a diverse romp across the French social and psychological landscape.

The actors in the series reflect the rich cultural backdrop of France today. The women portraying the three BFFs all hail from different parts of French society: Zita Hanrot (Elsa) has a Black Jamaican mother and a blond father from the North of France; Sabrina Ouazani (Charlotte) was born in France of Algerian parents; and Joséphine Draï (Émilie) is sometimes a blonde, sometimes a brunette European Frenchwoman. Despite, or maybe because of, their different interests and personalities, they form a surprisingly believable trio.

The show's title promises that many episodes will be centered on sex: Will Elsa be reunited with her sexist ex, Max, in his newly sensitive incarnation, or will she continue to have sex with the escort, Julio, for the duration? Will Antoine have an affair with the sexy nurse? Will he and Émilie ever have sex again now that things between them have grown stale? Is Julio's cross-dressing roommate, Romain/Adèle, gay or trans, and will they find a partner? Will Charlotte eventually settle for just one guy?

The most surprising aspect of getting hooked on *The Hookup*

Plan is that through all the sexy language and premises, we come to understand that the story turns mostly on romantic love—what makes for a fulfilling relationship?—and on women's friendships that endure through thick and thin. It also concludes that partners need not be the center of one's life and that some people don't need a partner in order to live out their dreams.

Although at least one critic opined that the series was already out of date when it first aired—sexual mores were evolving so quickly—the show does immerse viewers in a relatively recent French social world. What begins as an absurd set of premises ultimately raises some important questions about sex and love, French style.

What is the relationship between sex and love in the French imagination? Who knows? There are as many answers as there are people. But one thing is certain: if you believe in folk magic, you have a pretty good chance of being loved in France. When the French pluck daisy petals to see if they are loved by their crush, the rhyme goes like this: *Il m'aime, un peu, beaucoup, passionnément, à la folie, pas du tout* (He loves me, a little, a lot, passionately, madly, not at all).

Think about your chances in this felicitous system! Whereas in English, with "He loves me, he loves me not," you have a 50 percent success rate, in French, as you pluck off the petals, your chances shoot up to better than 83 percent. Since learning the French saying, not once have I reverted to the American method of amorous prognostication.

THE FRENCH GET THE LAST LAUGH
. . . AND THE FIRST

Il est de la nature humaine de penser sagement et d'agir d'une façon absurde.

(It is human nature to think wisely and act absurdly.)

—Anatole France

Humans have seemingly always tried to find humor during the grimmest of times—think of Boccaccio's bawdy and boisterous tales in the *Decameron*, set during the Black Death (the outbreak of bubonic plague) in the fourteenth century, or of British gallows humor during World War I. During the initial Covid-19 lockdown (called *le confinement* in France), the French had their own distinctive approach. Their online memes included the staff of a nursing home performing a silly line dance (duly masked), with the more ambulatory residents coming to their doors and dancing gleefully along. Others took more extensive measures to make people laugh. Olivier Guitel, who had wanted to become a clown without completely giving up his farm, found a way to form a small company that now travels from town to town. Becoming "Raoul Nitrate," a self-described *agriclown-teur*, this farmer-clown now delights audiences outdoors—and reports that he has never been happier. In Paris, the Théâtre de la Ville produced a comedy for the times, *Eros en confinement* (Eros During Lockdown). One of my favorite responses to entertainment during the pandemic was an early music group in the Hautes-Alpes that rehearsed and gave concerts in a barn, replete with cattle—as far as one can tell from the videos, *les vaches* (the cows) relished the music. The byline in the papers read cheekily, *"Un concert vachement sympa"* (a really nice concert). The contented bovine audience does evoke laughter.

More than a few philosophers—from Hobbes (it stems from a feeling of superiority) to Kant (it arises from an incongruity) to Freud (it is a release from repressed emotions)—have broached the origins of laughter. The French philosopher Henri Bergson dug deeper: In the context of evolution, he saw laughing as a response to the "mechanical inelasticity" of human behavior. If I slip on a banana peel, and you laugh, it's because I was incapable of adapting to those circumstances. (Think of the genre of "fail videos.") If we laugh at supercilious people, it is a punitive laughter—those characters do not contribute to the betterment of our species. Laughter is fundamentally human, Bergson reminds us. Even if we laugh at an animal or a hat, it is because of what is human in it or in its interactions with humans. Bergson also claims that laughter blocks out other emotions, such as pity, melancholy, and fear—which can be a godsend. Finally, laughter "is in need of an echo," creating social bonds among groups over shared experience. This part of Bergson's theory explains the many jokes of out-groups by in-groups, and vice versa.

Take the Belgians. In French humor, the Belgian stands in for the ignorant outsider (a role played, successively, in the United States by the Irish, the Polish, and blondes). Here's a notoriously bad example of a Belgian joke in France:

Q: How do you spot a Belgian in an airport?
A: He's the only one feeding breadcrumbs to the airplanes.
Q: How do you spot a Belgian airplane?
A: It's the only one eating the crumbs.

But the humor works both ways: "God created France, the most beautiful country in the world," as the Belgians tell it. "But knowing that others would be jealous, God did something to make it fair. He created the French."

One morning, I awoke with a start to the news, announced on the radio station France Inter, that after years of debate and conflict, Belgium had at last split into two separate states—one for French speakers (Walloons) and one for Flemish speakers (Flemings). *That's going to be a mess*, I thought. What would happen to all the shared spaces and government-funded services? How would those be divided, particularly in a place like Brussels, where both groups lived? I had read about growing problems between the two factions. To protest against the "linguistic imperialism" of French in Flanders (the Flemish-speaking regions of Belgium), safety warnings and other information had been posted in parks and elsewhere only in Flemish. In mixed areas, French- and Flemish-speaking students sometimes studied different curricula on separate floors of the same school. According to some reports, some pharmacies refused to fill prescriptions unless they were written in Flemish. "Long live free Flanders! May Belgium die!" was the war cry of the Flemish nationalist party.

Following the announcement of the country's definitive division or "partition," France Inter reported, Belgians took to the streets in ardent demonstrations, either for or against the partition . . . until news emerged that the report was *un poisson d'avril* (literally, "an April fish"), or an April Fool's Day prank.

I remember the announcement of the partition so clearly, and being shocked at the news before realizing that it was a joke. However, recently, when I went to the France Inter website to verify the prank, I saw that it had been played on the Belgians by a Belgian newscaster some *six months before* the newscast I heard. What France Inter had broadcast that April morning was not, as I had imagined, the station's own April Fool's joke, but rather a replay of a hoax that took place in Belgium several months earlier as though it were news—and I, and probably many other listeners, had fallen for it. We had been doubly April Fooled.

Other April Fool's pranks in France are much simpler—as when children make paper fish, sometimes crayon-colored in great detail, and surreptitiously tape them to the backs of children and adults alike. All those colorful fish taped on clothing make for a festive environment. The trick in elementary schools is to see how many fish can be taped to teachers' backs without their knowledge. Some teachers may even end up unknowingly taking the métro home with their backs embellished by brightly hued fish—a version of Joseph's coat of many colors.

If the Fish of April provide French children with a first taste of humor, then puppet theater must not be far behind. How do you hook small children into loving live theater? Paris has just the solution.

Nestled in the heart of the Jardin du Luxembourg, Les Guignols have performed for generations of children. Though the character of Guignol was created in Lyon in the nineteenth century, this particular puppet show was initiated in 1933 for the purpose of creating young French audiences who would later support the arts. (That's my interpretation, anyway.) But unlike in La Comédie Française and other more grown-up venues, audiences can talk back to the Guignols.

Watch out, Guignol!

No, don't go in there, Guignol!

The children adore the participatory element, and the humor is slapstick and easily understood. But the Guignols do not have American children in mind—that is, children unaccustomed to fairy tales that end in ways other than happily ever after. My daughters didn't know at the time that, in the original European tales, the wolf ends up eating both Little Red Riding Hood and her grandmother, Cinderella's stepsisters mutilate their feet to fit them into the glass slipper, and the Little Mermaid dies by suicide and becomes sea foam.

At first my daughters weren't prepared for the violence of this theater in the Jardin du Luxembourg, where puppets beat one other with clubs and where Guignol repeatedly pummeled police officers. However, much like cartoon characters who are flattened but pop back up, the assaulted puppets sprang back into action, and it soon became clear that the actions were harmless. Besides, the children are always on Guignol's side as they advise him, cajole him, and laugh with him.

Many stand-up comics of various origins in France today— Fary (Cape Verde); Fellag, Mohamed le Suédois, and Inès Reg (Algeria); Jamel Debbouze and Gad Elmaleh (Morocco); and Roukiata Ouedraogo (Burkina Faso)—play with the notion of cultural misunderstandings among groups, including their own. In his stand-up show called *Hexagone*, the comedian Fary notes that three adjectives best describe the French reputation: *impoli* (impolite), *râleur* (complaining), and most of all, *arrogant*—and both French- and Algerian-born audiences seem to love this caricature. But Fary goes further: For the French, the crosswalk is not a specific place—it's wherever you happen to place your foot. As for traffic lights: "Red, green—it's Christmas!" Personally, I appreciate being able to cross the street in the middle of a block if no cars are coming. In contrast, in Seattle, you can be arrested and given a life sentence for even attempting this transgression—or, at least that's how the natives treat the subject there. Being a pedestrian in France is liberating, albeit occasionally life-threatening.

French humor has been historically associated with societal issues, politics, and social class, and Inès Reg's humor is no exception. The Franco-Algerian Reg performed at Le Comedy Club in the 9th arrondissement of Paris before she became especially famous with a series of "Kevin" videos, in which she declares to "Kevin" that she wants more *paillettes* (glitter) in her life. When he responds that they can go out to McDo (pronounced "Mack Doh," French for "McDonald's"), she protests, saying that her fancy makeup alone cost thirty euros, so a four-euro McDo will most certainly *not* bring glitter into her life. After the whimsical Kevin videos, Reg's base mushroomed to over two million *fololos* (slang for "followers").

But Reg's funniest skits are found in a series of Instagram videos in which she declares her deep desire to be "Miss France" representing the "93," for Seine Saint Denis (probably the most culturally diverse suburb of Paris), which has never before entered a contestant in that pageant. She explains in a delightfully mock-sincere tone that it means everything to her to represent this wonderful *département* that has so many things to brag about, beginning with its multicultural population and its kebabs. It's clear that Reg's humor is not directed at her home, however, but at the absurd exercise of anyone competing to be called "Miss France."

Reg takes short, deliberate breaths, looking with wide

eyes into the camera and fidgeting uncomfortably as she tries to fashion her speech as she goes along. She repeatedly plows through the limits of the Instagram format, picking up in each new Instagram video exactly where she left off in the previous one. Her long speech is interrupted only by little blips connecting the videos and by her own hysterical exclamations when she thinks she has strayed from the persona she is creating. (*"Merde!* I didn't mean to say that! Is the mic working?"*) In an ironic twist, Reg later accepted the invitation to be a member of the jury for "Miss France 2022." My hunch is that her star will continue to rise.

I've only scratched the surface of the many comedians performing in France today, but their success demonstrates the power of comedy to address and sometimes heal cultural divides. When I went to a Fellag show in Bobigny (in the aforementioned "93"), about half the audience members were *maghrébins* (of North African origin) and half of European origin. It was gratifying to hear the laughter from all sides, whether the stereotypes foregrounded were Algerian or French. The Arab-speaking audience howled when Fellag threw in some Arab phrases while imitating members of his family. Those of us in the venue who were limited to French visibly enjoyed the others' delight, as we tried to fill in the blanks.

Rabelais said it best four centuries ago: *"Le rire est le propre de l'homme"* (with a little poetic license, "Laughter makes us human").

3

Sparking the Mind

Chaque question possède une force que la réponse ne contient plus.
(Every question possesses a force that the answer no longer contains.)
—Elie Wiesel

In most of the world, "sixth sense" refers to proprioception, or the sensation of where our bodies are in space—but I'm convinced that, in France, the sixth sense is the intellect. Despite Descartes's famous principle *"Cogito ergo sum"* (I think, therefore I am), the French continually incorporate the intellect into the physical world: carrying on a deep conversation over a meal, analyzing the texture of a contemporary painting, or discussing the musical cadence of a French popular song. Descartes, in his *Discours* on the scientific method of 1637, writes that what makes him truly himself (his *âme*, or "spirit," "soul," "consciousness") is entirely distinct from the body. The senses would tell us nothing, he argues, were it not for our *entendement* (understanding). But we could add that, in many cases, our understanding would be nil without the senses.

The paradox of the mathematician-philosopher's claim is

that he is incapable of writing about the intellect without resorting to terminology that evokes the body and the senses; vocabulary drawn from sight, hearing, smell, and touch figure in his treatise on method. Why? Because the French language uses words drawn from bodily experience to describe learning. *Sentir* means both "to smell" and "to feel"; *entendre* means "to hear" and "to understand"; and *voir* means "to see," both literally and figuratively. Even Descartes, the founding father of the mind/body distinction, implicitly (if unwittingly) demonstrates in his writing the continuum of the two forces.

The importance of the intellect in the French imagination is crystalized in Stendhal, one of the most celebrated novelists of the nineteenth century (along with Balzac, Flaubert, Hugo, and Zola). His iconic novel *The Red and the Black* features a well-rehearsed refrain in coming-of-age novels: a naïve, provincial boy goes to an exotic, scheming big city (in this case, Paris) and becomes corrupted. Stendhal's heroes share youthful energy, a search for passion and happiness, and enough cynicism to avoid sappiness. The protagonist of *The Red and the Black*, Julien Sorel, arrives in the rarified circles of the Marquis de Rênal to work as his secretary. In this world where social status centers on seeing and being seen, Julien, sensing his own inferiority, carefully observes all the classy guests at a dinner party. He is completely ignored except for a denigrating remark made by the marquis. Julien's upwardly mobile fate eventually becomes sealed, not by his new aristocratic clothes or his dancing lessons, but by a felicitous turn in the conversation to Latin. When he begins to answer pointed questions about the Latin poet Horace, it becomes clear that his knowledge far exceeds that of the dinner guests, who are suddenly intrigued and impressed by his intellectual assurance.

In this novel, as elsewhere in France, knowledge (*le savoir*) can be an entrée into higher social circles. Not all nineteenth-century French novels include such an emphasis on the intellect, but it is difficult to imagine English-speaking characters like David Copperfield or Huckleberry Finn advancing in their quests simply by knowing Latin!

My own trajectory has been nothing like Julien Sorel's. For starters, my Latin is atrocious. But in France, I have been able to come into contact with people that neither my birthright nor social circumstances would ever have allowed me to meet. The French sociologist Pierre Bourdieu invented the term *social capital* to describe various elements that allow individuals to exert power in society, including education. In that sense, you could argue that my being in a university setting has allowed me to cross paths with both Michel Foucault (historian and philosopher) and Julia Kristeva (literary critic and psychoanalyst) when I was a student, to take a public seminar with Pierre Bourdieu, to have a conversation with Eugène Ionesco (playwright) about teaching his plays, to chat with Jacques Derrida (I won't even try to define him!) after a lecture, to speak with Laurent Gaudé (writer) in a small bookstore in Montparnasse, and to hear Agnès Varda (filmmaker) speak about her film *The Gatherers* in the tiny Cinéma Saint André des Arts, in the Latin Quarter. Some of these figures may not be well known beyond France, but they are all intellectual and artistic giants in their own culture.

It is not only because I circulate in the world of students and teachers that I have had the opportunity to meet these figures. Many of these writers are "public intellectuals"—that is, they respond to interviews and give free lectures in auditoriums, libraries, and bookstores. Perhaps most surprising of all, they also regularly appear on national television and are featured on the radio, in podcasts, and on YouTube. Anyone who is interested

can usually gain access in some form to France's public intellectuals and artists—who seem to believe that, after accumulating
all their experience and knowledge, they are obliged to share it
with the masses.

A few years ago, I was attending a literary conference in
Rouen, where I was to give a lecture on the Renaissance-era explorer Jean de Léry. I accepted the invitation before I knew that
the famous author Pascal X—I've altered his surname slightly
to protect his privacy—would be the plenary speaker. We more
modest participants had been warned: Don't strike up long conversations with the hallowed author. He likes to be alone so
much that he scarcely uses email and usually refuses invitations.

Grateful that this luminary had deigned to come to our
meager scholarly gathering, we were instructed to address him
gingerly, with the requisite respect and distance. When the time
came for dinner at a long table, I, being one of only two foreign
scholars present, stepped back to allow more important participants to be seated first. At the end of that process, the only place
left at the table was immediately to the right of Pascal X. I was
then faced with a split-second decision: Was I having a severe
appendicitis attack that would force me to rush off, or should I
sit down next to him? The punk song "Should I Stay or Should
I Go?" by the Clash raced through my head. The chair was being pulled out for me, so evidently, the die had been cast. As I
slipped into my seat, I looked left, where a pair of piercing blue
eyes faced mine.

"*Bonsoir,*" I offered, unable to think of a better way to begin
a conversation.

It turns out that when you speak with Pascal X, you are
the only person in the room. Our topics drifted from literature
to politics to contemporary culture. At some points during the

dinner, he turned to others who were eagerly awaiting his attention, but then he would inevitably turn back to me, and we would resume where we had left off.

When the dinner was over and the bus came to the restaurant to take us back to the hotel across town, Pascal X asked me if I'd like to walk back to the hotel with him. I love almost nothing better than long walks and hikes—so, off we went. As we walked for several kilometers, we heard in the distance a jazz group playing outdoors. There was vibrancy in the air.

During that stroll, Pascal X explained to me that he rises at four or four thirty every morning to write; that he loves that time of day, when the world is silent and he can work in solitude; that no one ever interrupts him at that hour; and that all his books began in those circumstances; that he would never have imagined that his book would be made into a film; that he relished time alone, never seeking out big gatherings, and that small exchanges brought him great pleasure.

I asked if, given the late hour, he would rise at four the next morning to write.

Probably, he replied.

We reached the hotel, which was by this time completely dark. The distant music had died out, and we each returned quietly to our rooms, trying not to make noise on the stairs. As I lay down in bed, I felt the kind of quiet joy I associate with privileged and profound exchanges, however brief.

The next day, as I began my talk, I looked all around the auditorium, wondering if Pascal X was there. Maybe he and I could continue our conversation of the night before; he could comment on my thesis about the representation of cannibals as metaphor. I would love to hear his thoughts on the subject.

About halfway through the talk, I spotted him in the audience—he was there!

Yes, Pascal X was there . . . *nodding off in the back row.*

My plan had obviously bombed, but this didn't take away from the fact that meetings of minds, the great minds and not so great, is such a common occurrence in France that you might be tempted to take such happenings for granted. But I don't. Pick up a paper, flip on the television, tune in for a podcast, or eavesdrop on a conversation in a café, and your mind will likely be stimulated.

Francis Bacon famously argued that "knowledge is power," but in France, knowledge can also be fabulously fun.

SAVORING BOOKS

On aime toujours un peu à sortir de soi, à voyager, quand on lit.
(We always like to get outside of ourselves, to travel, when we read.)
　　　　　　　　　　　　　　　　　　　　—Marcel Proust

My favorite bookshop in Paris is postage-stamp tiny, and not far from the Montparnasse train station. The door to the shop, as with many older shops in Paris, opens inward. Visitors in the know open it carefully because, depending on the weather, they might run into the rotating postcard and greeting card display stand. The owner of the shop, Sophie, has seemingly read every book on the shelves and is happy to discuss your interests with you. If you say, "I'm looking for a book that . . ." she will find it for you. Sophie is a fierce proponent of independent booksellers and hosts many readings, signings, and exchanges with writers.

Like coffee shops in Seattle, bookstores pepper the landscape throughout Paris. For centuries, France has developed a culture of readers, of everything from medieval legends to contemporary crime fiction. A recent study by the International Publishers Association found that France publishes 60 percent more books per capita than the United States. What always strikes me is the extent to which reading happens in the public sphere in France. Even if you haven't read particular books, you'll learn about them through conversations with friends, while listening to popular podcasts, or even from posters in the métro or at bus stops. Reading might appear to be a solitary endeavor, but in France it's a social activity; everyone seems to be doing it. By delving into books, you connect with others. Many world cultures engage in reading and debates, of course, but somehow, France has cultivated a public and interactive culture of readers who discuss books over coffee and on park benches. Like friendship, reading in France is meant to be savored and shared. "Do not read as children do, to enjoy themselves, or as the ambitious do, to educate themselves," wrote Gustave Flaubert. "No, read to live."

Americans always want happy endings, as we learn in the popular Netflix series *Emily in Paris*. The show often plays with both French and American stereotypes—it flaunts them, brandishes them, embraces them—but rarely negates them: Emily dresses in bright, flashy clothes as contrasted with the subtle blacks and grays of her French counterparts. She barges into conversations with spontaneous, daring ideas, whereas her French colleagues are more cerebral and reserved. Emily would like to find a suitable boyfriend, while her French colleagues sleep with one another's husbands and wives.

At one telling moment, Emily's Einstein-resembling colleague, Luc, asserts, "American romantic comedies are so dishonest. We would like more of a French ending."

"Which is what?" Emily asks.

Luc's colleague Julien dramatically responds, "Tragic."

"More like life," Luc adds. "He dies or loses a limb, or she prefers to be a lesbian—which happens."

"Yeah, happy endings are very American," Julien offers.

"But they give you hope," Emily retorts. "And the hero wins in the end. Don't you want to see the hero win?"

"No," Luc replies emphatically. "I want to see life, the hero tortured for his love . . . and the actress naked." (Could a Frenchman be more stereotyped than this?)

"But don't you want to go to the movies to escape life?" Emily counters.

"Thinking that you can escape life is your problem. You can never escape life. Never," Luc intones.

"Welcome to the French ending," Julien announces, as both men turn and walk away.

My students have occasionally made similar claims about French literature and its propensity for complexity, melancholy, and death. As with most clichés, there's at least some truth to the claim, but the works are far more fascinating than what first meets the eye. Take one of the most famous French novels, *Madame Bovary*. (Spoiler alert: skip the rest of this paragraph and the next three if you haven't yet read any of these works.) Yes, Emma Bovary puts an end to her life of drudgery and despair—as contrasted with the luminous one of her imagination—but the novel doesn't end there. It ends not with darkness, but with irony, as the inept pharmacist Monsieur Homais receives the Legion of Honor.

Or consider Victor Hugo's *The Hunchback of Notre Dame*, which, in decrying the treatment of "gypsies" and the disabled, is filled with great humanity. In a wonderful example of art inspiring life, the publication of Hugo's novel in 1831 also spurred the complete restoration of Notre Dame Cathedral.

And then there's Voltaire's satirical *Candide*, a biting takedown of optimism and positivism if ever there was one. Yes, among other trials, Candide faces deadly weather, the Lisbon earthquake, and war. Matters could scarcely be worse in "the best of all possible worlds." But what is the exhortation of the novel's last line? *"Il faut cultiver notre jardin"* (We must cultivate our garden). Many a truth is spoken in irony, and the Enlightenment-era belief in knowledge for the common good can be seen peeking through Candide's clouds.

And what about Camus's *The Stranger*? Yes, the novel ends on the verge of Meursault's execution, but paradoxically, he realizes "that he had been happy, that he is happy again." To consummate the final act and to feel less alone, he hopes that a large crowd will greet him with cries of hatred. Yet readers understand that the crowd will not have triumphed over Meursault. Instead, he will be liberated, freed from all expectations.

All these endings are multilayered, inviting further reflection in a way that "happily ever after" could only wish for. To alter Tolstoy's claim from *Anna Karenina* only slightly—happy endings are all alike, but every ambiguous ending is ambiguous in its own fascinating way.

LINGERING IN LIBRARIES

With more than forty million cataloged works, the Bibliothèque nationale de France (the National Library) boasts one of the largest collections in the world. The old Bibliothèque nationale building is breathtakingly gorgeous. Under stately metal domes with numerous skylights, the main reading room, with its wooden tables and soft yellow reading lamps, looks as though time stopped there in the nineteenth century—which, save for the electric light fixtures and the now-digitized card catalog, it did.

As you sit at one of the circular tables, you are surrounded by curved rows of books that call out to you but that you cannot pull off the shelves. You must know exactly which ones you want and order them from the library staff. In earlier times, we filled out elaborate duplicate yellow forms for each book request, and if you didn't press hard enough so that the second sheet was exactly as dark as the first, or if a single detail was missing, the unflinching library staff would make you fill out the form again. Today, gloriously, all books can be requested online in advance.

When I was a student, I learned that, at the end of the day, you could set aside the books you were working on and save them for a maximum of three days, so I tentatively asked a staff member if I could save the books I was using until the next morning.

"Oui," he responded curtly. "Where is your *sangle*?"

My sangle? I thought. *Um,* sanglier *means "boar," but that's probably not what he means . . .*

The librarian impatiently pulled out a canvas lanyard and showed it to me: "Oui, un *sangle*."

It turns out that it was *impossible* (a word that often comes up

in French administrative situations) to save the books without a *sangle*. So, the books I needed were lost for that day.

The next day, after a trip to a bookstore to acquire a *sangle*, I requested the same books and, at the end of the day, went to turn them in, this time with my *sangle* safely buckled around them.

"*Non*," the same gruff staff member said, "you must have your *name* written on the *sangle*." Even though all the carefully filled-out forms accompanied the stack of books, it was *impossible* for him to accept it without a name written on the *sangle*.

After working diligently to trace over the pen marks on the lanyard enough times to make them legible, I tried again to turn in the books, but no. It turns out that you needed to write the name several times so that it would be visible on the lanyard from all angles.

After much more coloring in of the letters, I triumphantly

turned in my stack of books, with duplicate forms, with the *sangle*, and with my name writ large. The attendant seized the stack of books and slid it onto the shelf without blinking, refusing to acknowledge that I had at last mastered the system.

There would be no celebrating in the National Library that day. But I, drunk with victory, smiled all the way to the métro.

The old National Library had strict rules in other areas as well. One day in late October, it was freezing outside and only slightly warmer inside. Most of us kept our coats on while we worked, and by midday, our fingers having turned blue, we put on gloves, too—which, as you can imagine, made it rather difficult to turn the pages of books and write or type. When I finally asked someone at the espresso machine why the place was so cold, she replied, "Don't you know? The government doesn't allow the heat to be turned on in its buildings until November first."

Wow. Indeed, in November, on a nice, warm day, the heat was turned up so high that all of us, including the library staff, were peeling off layer after layer, languishing as if it were a searing summer day. But those were the rules.

The most unpleasant employee at the old National Library was the woman who tended the *vestiaire* (the coat check). Dressed in a white blouse, a drab pencil skirt, and unremarkable pumps, she was of indeterminate age (fifty going on ninety?). Readers could not take coats into the reading room, not even if they were small, unassuming, and flattened, like mine. No, you had to wait in line to check your coat every morning, and even the friendliest "Bonjour" would scarcely win you a glance from the clerk, who glared at all the patrons as though each of us was completely ruining her day (as she was simultaneously beginning to ruin ours).

I tried everything with her:

"*Vous allez bien?*" (How are you doing?)

"*Il fait frisquet aujourd'hui, non?*" (It's a little chilly today, don't you think?)

These useless pleasantries continued for several months. Then Christmas season rolled around, and I began to wonder: *What will it take to get this woman out of her funk?* The only thing I could think of was to make her a batch of Christmas cookies—that approach sometimes works to cheer up Americans, but would such a gesture move this Frenchwoman? When I had made oatmeal date cookies for my French family a few years before, they had politely declared them *intéressants* (a French euphemism for "disgusting"), and the frankest and youngest brother mercilessly noted that they reminded him of dog food. Would plain sugar cookies be a safe bet for the dour woman at the *vestiaire?*

One morning, I mustered up my courage, baked some cookies, and brought them to the library in a pretty holiday bag. When I handed them to the woman in the *vestiaire*, I said simply, "*C'est pour vous. Joyeux Noël!*" (These are for you. Merry Christmas!)

Heaven and earth moved, and the woman smiled—a real smile. "*Merci. C'est gentil.*" (Thank you. That's nice.)

While those may be among the only words spoken to me besides something like a brief "*Ils étaient bons*" (They were good) in January, it's not an overstatement to say that her demeanor was transformed. Every morning, the dour look would morph into the smallest *Mona Lisa* smile, and my life on the planet became a bit more pleasant for the rest of my time at the National Library. Like the celebrated German-English truce laced with rum on the battlefields on Christmas Eve 1914, wouldn't it be fantastic if these microcosmic moments of sharing were transferrable to the macrocosm?

Most of the collection at the old National Library (also known as the BN, for "Bibliothèque Nationale"), on the rue de Richelieu near the Palais Royal, has now been moved to the hyper-modern Bibliothèque François Mitterrand, France's tribute to one of its most popular twentieth-century presidents. Today, the old library building still houses manuscripts (along with books about music and art; letters, medals, and coins), but the more than fifteen million books needed a larger home. A friend of mine thought that the new library was really cool because the buildings that make it up look like the legs of an upside-down table, but they were designed by Dominique Perrault, fittingly, to represent four open books. The buildings appear to be completely separate as seen from the esplanade, but underground, they are connected by a vast series of reading rooms, halls, and lobbies. The lowest level is reserved for researchers, and up a flight of concealed stairs is a closely guarded room where the rarest books are stored.

The first time I worked in the rare books room, I was in heaven—though it had been hellish to get in. Before you're admitted, you have to put all your personal items in a locker, except for a laptop, paper, and a pencil, if you'd like (no pens allowed). You then fill out forms to justify in great detail your reason for consulting each book, a rule made to protect each from undue wear. Sometimes you need to negotiate with the head librarian. I don't usually admit this in public, but when, after long justifications, I finally held in my hands the first edition of Pierre de Ronsard's poetry collection *Les Amours* (1552), I had to swallow several times—it was too beautiful.

Careful! I silently yelled to myself. *No tears on the book!*

I couldn't believe my good fortune—to hold a sixteenth-century book with the stamp of the king's library on it: BIBLIOTHÈQUE ROYALE. Henry II may have held this very book in his hands, or Marie Stuart, or Ronsard himself! Turning those ancient pages, I was transported to the Renaissance and could almost hear lutes and shawms in the distance.

But the rules of the rare books room don't apply only to the treatment of its books. They extend to patron behavior. I learned this one day after a long afternoon of research, when I leaned my head against my hand to contemplate my notes. Suddenly, a guard appeared at my side: *"Mademoiselle, on ne dort pas ici"* (You can't sleep here).

"Je ne dormais pas" (I wasn't sleeping), I replied. *"Je pensais"* (I was thinking).

Still, as every hassled library patron must allow, even the gruffest National Library employees have the same serious purpose: It is their mission to protect one of France's most valuable legacies—books that can take a reader to worlds and times unknown, as the works of Charles Baudelaire, Michel de Montaigne, and Marguerite Duras have done for me.

SLEEPING WITH BAUDELAIRE

I had probably been in love before, once. Okay, maybe twice. But my first *true* love was Baudelaire.

It all began when our literature teacher at the Sorbonne required us to memorize a sonnet—which, it turns out, is common practice in French schools, beginning at an early age. Learning poetry, we were told, develops the ability to think metaphorically and to appreciate the sonorous beauties of the French language, blah blah blah.

Fine. So I began to read aloud Baudelaire's 1857 poem "Correspondences" (rendered here in English): "Nature is a temple in which living pillars . . ." Living pillars . . . Trees, right? . . . "sometimes emit mystical words . . ." I became lost in this forest of symbols and musical syllables, realizing that the word *correspondences* referred to objects, yes, but also to sounds and to the senses.

It was love at first sight. Baudelaire and I quickly began to read poems together—at least in my imagination. *To recite a French sonnet,* he insisted, *you can't pause or breathe just anywhere. The voice must be continuous until the end of the phrase, as if you are playing a musical instrument.* He said that the sonnet was "Pythagorean"—in the tiniest of things, you can find the greatest beauty. I remember the image he used to describe a sonnet: the most glorious view of the firmament is seen not from a mountaintop, but as a slice of sky between two rooftops. The sonnet must be *économique,* and every syllable counts. Baudelaire's sonorous vowels reminded me of a poem I had read aloud many times as a child: Edgar Allan Poe's "Annabel Lee."

> *And neither the angels in Heaven above*
> *Nor the demons down under the sea*
> *Can ever dissever my soul from the soul*
> *Of the beautiful Annabel Lee;*
> *. . .*
> *And so, all the night-tide, I lie down by the side*
> *Of my darling—my darling—my life and my bride,*
> *In her sepulcher there by the sea*
> *In her tomb by the sounding sea.*

Not realizing that a childhood crush could have any relationship to a mature and authentic love, I didn't know at the time that my new lover, Baudelaire, had spent seventeen years translating Poe's poetry.

Baudelaire was also the one who taught me about synesthesia, a correspondence and confusion of the senses that is technically a medical condition but that translates into a fantastically sensuous overload in his sonnet, "Correspondances." Late in the evening, Baudelaire would recite to me, in his mellifluous tones, verses about green prairies and the sweet sounds of oboes. Scents of amber, musk, and balsamic resin lulled us to sleep.

A "friend" of Baudelaire's, personified Beauty (*La Beauté*), occasionally came between us. He was obsessed by her and even wrote several poems for her. She had not been his lover, really—but, as they say, it's complicated. She was hardened and stately, *comme un rêve de pierre* (like a dream of stone). At least, that's how B. described her. Mostly, she liked to imagine herself immortal. I suspected that she might move in with my poet someday. Like the soil where Sauvignon blanc grapes grow, Beauty had minerality in her soul, as she herself admitted: *Et jamais je ne pleure, et jamais je ne ris* (Never do I cry, and never do I laugh). Much of her time was spent with her mirrors, and when you looked through them, everything appeared more beautiful (*De purs miroirs qui font toutes choses plus belles*). I guess B.'s relationship with her could be described as "love/hate"—he seemed both to desire and to resent her, while I looked on.

And then there were Baudelaire's cats (*les chats*), which appear amply in his poems. It's no small matter to be able to get along with your partner's pets. Baudelaire's cats were magical, powerful, and gentle (*puissants et doux*), not docile. Like aging lovers and austere scholars, they were solitary creatures. Had they not been so proud, they could have been messengers for Erebus, the god of shadows and the passage to the underworld. Like sphinxes, they reigned over . . . well, everything. Anyone could get lost in their mystical eyes, with their pupils radiating outward like fine sand (*un sable fin*).

To put it briefly, the cats and I bonded. Probably because of this unbreakable attachment between the cats and me, Baudelaire and I never officially split up. It was, rather, a natural drifting. The years went by, and we simply found ourselves living different lives—though I still occasionally recite his poetry to the family cat.

After my affair with Baudelaire, other French literary lovers entered my world—Ronsard, Racine, Hugo, Michel Deguy, Louise Labé. And why not? In France, polyamory is in the air. But Baudelaire still has a hold over me that no other lover can subsume. His heightened sensuality, his frenemy Beauty, and the memory of his inscrutable cats continue to accompany me on my journey—and in my fantasies.

EXPLORING WITH MONTAIGNE

If I could take just one thick book to a deserted island, Montaigne's *Essays* from the sixteenth century would be it. This book takes readers on a trip into Montaigne's mind and body—and into their own. The essayist sees life as continually in flux, with the only constant being inconstancy. In keeping with the French focus on water, he seems to delight in the water as it flows around his feet. His essays are filled with maxims and pithy, quotable lines that could be construed as lessons. But Montaigne isn't preaching—he's sharing with readers something that has dawned on him or that he has been mulling over for a while. *"Je n'enseigne point, je raconte"* (I don't teach, I tell [stories]), he assures us. His ideas are sometimes complex, but they come to us cloaked in good-natured humor and teasing. Volumes have been and will again be written on Montaigne's thoughts, but for our purposes, what does he have to say about finding joy?

Some forty years after Montaigne's death, in what is now known as the *cogito* (mentioned earlier), Descartes would claim that the body and the mind are separate entities. Montaigne speaks much more to twenty-first-century audiences than does Descartes when he argues that the body and the soul or the self cannot be conceived of as separate entities, with only a "narrow seam" between them. In this same spirit, Montaigne declares in his autobiographical essays his wish to paint himself "*entier, et tout nud*" (completely, and entirely naked). His focus on the body as a marker of our humanity continues throughout the essays. As you read them, it's as though the author were inviting you to a fireside discussion with him, glass of wine in hand.

"If I had to live again, I would live as I have lived," Montaigne writes, as the ultimate act of acceptance. Some see this attitude as a cop-out, arguing that Montaigne was reluctant to shake things up. Others see him as a hero for being able to let go of what could not be; as "the freest and mightiest of souls," as Nietzsche described him. But I see Montaigne as falling between these two extremes, and as someone who is constantly revising what he thinks. His manuscripts bear out this claim: when he begins to write a new edition of his essays, he doesn't delete ideas; he simply adds to them, along the lines of "on the other hand" or "you could also say that . . ." In the essays, we observe the evolution of Montaigne's philosophy, and we understand almost viscerally that no human thought can be fixed in time.

We don't make enough space for pleasure in our lives, Montaigne writes in an essay on drunkenness. While he rejects drunkenness on the principle that it is vital always to have control over our consciousness and our being, he subscribes to Plato's claim that wine gives temperance to the soul and health to the body, grants older people the courage to dance, and makes everyone merrier. He does, however, include a disclaimer: military men, judges, and magistrates should not engage in drinking when they are carrying out their duties. The funniest of Montaigne's remarks in his chapter on drinking is his belief that the French are too fussy about the quality of their wines. If your pleasure depends on drinking good wine, he warns, you condemn yourself to the disappointment of sometimes drinking bad wine. The Germans, he says, have a much better approach: They drink all wines with equal pleasure. (Could this Frenchman possibly be suggesting that the Germans settle for less?)

"Of Experience" is my favorite Montaigne essay, and here we see a Renaissance man explaining joie de vivre as he lived it, with experience as his teacher. The essayist relishes what he calls the *épaisseur* (thickness) of time as he focuses on just one thing. In contemporary lingo, that concept might translate into "mindfulness." "When I sleep, I sleep. When I dance, I dance," he writes. And when he goes for a walk, his thoughts wander, but then he brings them back to the walk itself, to the orchard, to the sweetness of solitude, and to himself. If you are constantly multitasking, as I am, this kind of concentration may inspire you.

At the end of his multivolume work, Montaigne leaves us with a fitting image of the humanity embodied in his writings: *"Et au plus eslevé throne du monde si ne sommes assis que sus nostre cul."* (And on the loftiest throne in the world, we are still sitting on our own bums). When someone complains, "I have done nothing today," Montaigne counters, "What? Have you not lived? That is not only the principal but also the most illustrious of your occupations." He rues our tendency to describe an activity as a *passe-temps* (pastime), as though time were something to be avoided or ignored. "I do not want to pass the time," he writes. "I savor it, I cling to it . . . I find it both pleasant and valuable, even in its last decline, as in my current condition . . . We have only ourselves to blame if it weighs on us and if it escapes us without our taking advantage of it." Time, in other words, is the finest gift of our existence. In this essay, Montaigne articulates French attitudes that prevail to the present day: Make the moment last. It is within our power to find our own "thickness" in time.

DELIGHTING IN DURAS

I came to Marguerite Duras's writings with trepidation; I had heard that her work was impossible to read. Duras was the darling of the intellectual and cinematic worlds of the twentieth century, having written works ranging from the "new novel" *Moderato cantabile* to the script for the 1959 film *Hiroshima mon amour*. But in addition to her experimental writings, Duras also published something much more accessible: an autobiographical work, *L'Amant* (*The Lover*), which proceeded to win the most coveted literary honor in France, the Prix Goncourt. Written in sparing yet poetic French prose, the work is simply a sumptuous read. It is one of those rare stories that end perfectly. Upon my first reading of the book, when I got to the last page, I read it and then read it again. And, each time, I became more convinced: it was a magnificent ending.

The story is set in 1930s Vietnam, where Duras's widowed mother is a teacher and where the young Marguerite and her two brothers are being raised in near poverty. As a teenager, Marguerite becomes involved with a wealthy Chinese man twelve years her senior. Recounted in the first and third person (*je/elle*), the narration is neither fluid nor linear. The book implicitly raises questions about colonial-era interactions among Vietnamese, Chinese, and French and the complexity of social standing, financial motivation, education, sexual attraction, and familial relations.

As there is little in this book that could be described as joyous, why would I include it in a book of reflections on joie de vivre? Because it is a stupendous read. Just as there is *Joy of Cooking* and *The Joy of Sex*, this book exemplifies *The Joy of Reading French Prose*—and there are also enough historical references and sex scenes to interest those not easily borne away by stunning writing. Valéry said that poetry is to prose what dance is to walking, but sometimes prose, too, can dance. I am incapable of reproducing the beauty of *L'Amant* here. Excerpts are rarely fulfilling, especially in translation—but here are a few characteristic examples for your contemplation:

> Early in my life it was too late. At eighteen, it was already too late. I had already grown old.

> My hair is heavy, supple, tender, a copper mass that falls below my shoulder blades. They often tell me that my hair is the loveliest thing about me, which I interpret to mean that I am not pretty.

> He is in an abominable love. Crying, he does it. First, there is pain. And then afterward, this pain is in turn taken, changed, slowly pulled away, transported toward pleasure, embraced in pleasure. The ocean, formless, simply incomparable.

> She doesn't know she's beautiful, Hélène Lagonelle . . . She. Hélène L. Hélène Lagonelle.

Note, in that final quote, the splendid repetition of the *el* sound: "*Elle ne sait pas qu'elle est très belle, Hélène Lagonelle . . .*

Elle." The internal rhyme of this last passage mesmerizes any reader who is listening, with *"elle/belle"* echoing in the mind, while the assonance of the *è* sound poetically carries the paragraph. The writer's obsession with Hélène Lagonelle is translated into sinuous sound.

It would be unfair not to mention that Duras's style has been the brunt of many literary parodies, along the lines of Hemingway's imagined explanation of why the chicken crossed the road: "To die. In the rain. Alone." I have even asked my students to write a pastiche of Duras, an assignment they particularly relish. But underneath that analytical cloak that professors often don, I was moved by this book, as were many of my students. It encapsulates the joy of language as the human body—in its sensual awakening, its vulnerability, and its force—comes to life on the page.

READING IN NATURE

During the summer after the first wave of the coronovirus pandemic, the city of Paris sponsored cultural events throughout the metropolitan area, all subsidized by the government: dance, theater, readings, concerts. Proof of vaccination was required for all activities, both indoors and out, but otherwise, everyone was invited.

When I arrived in Paris for the first time in two years on a July afternoon, I deposited my bags in my rented room and immediately headed out for a *lecture sous les arbres* (reading under the trees) in a garden just off the Champs Élysées at Place de la Concorde. It was free and open to the public.

The makeshift wooden stage surrounded an expansive linden tree, and our seating area of folding chairs was bordered by a delightfully unruly hedge. A quiet fountain hummed in the background. Thibault de Montalembert, an actor who is enjoying a spike in fame due to his role in the series *Dix pour cent* (Ten Percent; the title in English is *Call My Agent*), was reading from Florence Aubenas's recently released novel, *L'Inconnu de la poste* (The Stranger at the Post Office). The director of the Théâtre de la Ville had introduced the series by reminding us that reading was "*le don le plus précieux qui soit*" (the most precious gift that exists). Leaves gently stirred, sunshine appeared in the interstices of the leaves, and a kind breeze mollified the sun on my arms. As Montalembert read from the text—"*L'air vibrait de chaleur*" (the air vibrated with warmth)—I realized that this was yet another example of life imitating art.

Now fully committed to these "readings under the trees," I returned the next day to the same location. In the garden, the renowned actor Irène Jacob was reading from a book by Édouard Louis, *Combats et métamorphoses d'une femme* (English title: *A Woman's Battles and Transformations*), in which he recounts the "liberation" of his mother—liberation from poverty, from a horrible marriage, from small-town life, and from mind-numbing work. Jacob read a passage in which the gay son wants to reveal his sexuality to his mother without hurting her. We heard of his suffering both socially and emotionally. In the audience, a middle-aged blond woman in the second row pulled out a tissue and wiped her eyes.

Jacob recited the aphorisms that Édouard Louis learned as a child:

Chien qui a mordu, mordra. (A dog that has bitten, will bite.)

La pauvreté n'empêche pas la propreté. (Poverty doesn't prevent cleanliness.)

Méfie-toi du loup qui dort. (Beware of the sleeping wolf.)

"Je suis devenu un transfuge de classe par vengeance," Jacob continued reading. (I became a class defector out of vengeance.)

A man with a shaved head slouched backward in his chair, his arms folded over his chest, seemingly absorbed. He was wearing glasses with tortoiseshell frames, and his gray flowered shirt inched up, revealing the bottom part of his belly. A young woman wearing an African headband and a turquoise V-neck shirt had what the French call *"un beau décolleté"* (a nice plunging neckline) and black leather sandals. Her gaze was focused as she leaned toward the wooden stage, her eyes alert and intense.

As I observed the audience at this outdoor haven, I imagined that each person there was harboring some pain or secret sorrow. Emily Dickinson's "I measure every Grief I meet" came to mind. And yet—and yet—all present were listening to the reader with their entire bodies, as if they had come miles in the desert to drink cool water at an oasis. Readers and listeners were united under the trees, experiencing together the pleasure of beautifully poignant words.

SEEING THE LIGHT

Illumination is a "lightmotif," a thread running through French history. Light evokes both physical and metaphorical openness—discovery, clarity, a sense of joy. While the French cannot claim to have built the first light source for wayfaring sailors, Augustin-Jean Fresnel did in fact revolutionize the concept of the lighthouse with the invention, in 1822, of a lens using both refraction and reflection. Bending the light rays into one powerful beam, the Fresnel lens was "the invention that saved a million ships." If you've ever seen one, you know what a work of beauty it is. A conical miracle of glass that takes on and reflects all the colors around it, it was capable of projecting light many times as far as had previously been possible. The first Fresnel lens was installed in France's oldest lighthouse, the Cordouan Lighthouse, near Royan, on the Atlantic coast, where it is still in operation. While many Fresnel lenses have been replaced or augmented with electronic systems, the lighthouse keepers at Cordouan still wind the original clockwork assembly that rotates their lighthouse's lenses. Declared by UNESCO a World Heritage Site in 2021, this monument is a tribute to the dazzling alchemy of light.

Other French scientists have been instrumental, so to speak, in making discoveries pertaining to light. In the nineteenth century, Étienne-Louis Malus's experiments in light refraction led to the Malus Law of polarization; and François Arago devised an experiment to illustrate light wave theory. Joseph Nicéphore Niépce developed heliography (a technique using light to imprint a solvent-treated plate), which led to photography. The Lumière (Light) brothers brought about the birth of motion pictures with their invention of the "cinematograph," a revolutionary projector and camera. In 1895, the urban planner Georges-Eugène Haussmann installed thousands of gas street lamps in Paris, which made the city safer and its residents more prone to engage in nightlife. Haussmann reportedly said,

"De la lumière avant toute chose" (Light above all else). Some historians have argued that Haussmann's goal in designing vast boulevards was their efficacy in allowing Napoleon III's army to stamp out insurrections. Haussmann's own writings, how-

ever, seem to indicate that clearing the space for health and aesthetic reasons (to foreground statues and monuments) was his principal objective. Perhaps both theories are accurate.

Does Paris's status as the "City of Light" (Ville Lumière) come from the early profusion of streetlamps? Today, most of Paris's bridges, monuments, and boulevards are illuminated after nightfall, and the Eiffel Tower provides its own extravagant light show. Others claim that the nickname comes from the fact that Paris was lighted as early as the seventeenth century, when Nicolas de La Reynie, the lieutenant general of the police under Louis XIV, ordered all property owners to place lamps in their windows facing the street, to reduce crime. Still others contend that the nickname celebrates the brilliant intellectual "lights" of the Enlightenment, with Paris as the center for European education and ideas. Whatever the etymology may be, and despite the ecological reduction of hours that Parisian monuments will be illuminated, the city remains famously luminous. A German critic offered another explanation for the French passion for light: they are afraid of the dark.

The Enlightenment provides another window into the important role that light has played in the French imagination. Adam Gopnik cleverly sums up *le siècle des Lumières* (the Enlightenment) in a few words: "liberty, freedom of speech, religious tolerance, an embrace of science, erotic curiosity." Not too bad for a bird's-eye view! The eighteenth century was indeed a period of sexual experimentation and literary daring. However, "erotic curiosity" is a generous way to describe Le Marquis de Sade (from whose name the word *sadism* derives) and Laclos's novel *Dangerous Liaisons*, which combines sexual escapades with cleverness

and cruelty. Sade was admired by some twentieth-century thinkers, notably the forerunner to second-wave feminism, Simone de
Beauvoir. How could a pioneering feminist embrace the works
of a man who reveled in the torture of women? It's a bit more
complex than that, but ultimately, Beauvoir praises Sade's liberty from convention and his resistance to power. Denis Diderot
might be a better example of the Enlightenment's "erotic curiosity," notably his first novel, *Les Bijoux indiscrets* (translated as
The Indiscreet Toys). *Bijoux* was eighteenth-century slang for female
genitalia, but a synopsis of how in Diderot's novel genitals acquire the magic power to confess the relations they have had (!)
is beyond the purview of this book.

The Swiss writer Jean-Jacques Rousseau, also among the luminaries of the eighteenth century, is probably best known for
The Social Contract and *A Discourse on Inequality*, both of which
presage the French Revolution. His *Confessions* are considered
the first modern autobiography in French. But Rousseau's *Reveries of the Solitary Walker*, his final and unfinished work, speaks the
most directly to joie de vivre.

Having withdrawn from society, Rousseau details his walks
in the woods as he relishes a communion with nature. "The
practice of going into myself makes me lose the feeling—and
even the memory—of my troubles," he writes. On the Île Saint
Pierre, in Lake Bienne, not far from the border between Switzerland and France, he discovers the joy of solitary walking,
taking in all the different species of flora without ever wishing
to be elsewhere. He feels *ravissements* and *extases* (raptures and
ecstasies), a perfect and fulfilled contentment, as he drifts into
reveries during his walks or while lying in a rocking boat or
sitting on the banks of the lake watching waves. These flowery
pages point to the romantic writings that would soon be in

vogue in France, but again, Rousseau situates his happiness in the present, far from busyness and bustling.

The Swiss thinker bequeathed to France not only his writings, which have enlightened students for many generations, but also a sense of wonder and contentedness that can be found by turning inward, especially in nature. When I read the *Rêveries* at age nineteen, I loved the romantic reflections on humanity in nature; when my students now read the text at the same age, they see an invitation to think ecologically and to unplug temporarily from a highly technological world.

The most significant publishing event of the Enlightenment was not one of these novels and autobiographical essays, however, but a series of books that changed the world: the *Encyclopédie* (*Encyclopedia, or Reasoned Dictionary of Sciences, Arts, and Trades*), in twenty-eight volumes, edited under the direction of Denis Diderot. The importance of this publication cannot be overstated. It is an awe-inspiring compilation, with over a thousand illustrations—maps as well as demonstrations of "how things work." But more important, even though only about half the population could read when the *Encyclopédie* was published, this work began the process of democratizing knowledge. No longer would books containing troves of wisdom lie only in monasteries, in royal circles, and in the homes of nobles. Should you ever have the opportunity to see an early edition of this work in a rare books room of a library, seize it! Each volume is a marvel—a compendium of knowledge that had never before been available publicly. My college has a magnificent early edition of the *Encyclopédie* in its library. Students are dazzled by the foldout "Tree of Knowledge," which attempts to classify all disciplines from the three main branches, Memory/History, Imagination/Poetry, and Reason/Philosophy, reaching outward to numerous leaves ranging from pharmacy to diplomacy to vocal music. It's humbling to see this expanse of knowledge that reached so many and to imagine the continuing process of "illuminating" the public that it set in motion.

The Atelier des Lumières in Paris is a contemporary monument to light. While light shows now take place all over the world against the façades of cathedrals, in museums, and in other public spaces, I think that a tribute to the permanent "Studio of Light" is in order.

First, the venue: Created in 1835, the immense foundry of Chemin Vert produced quality parts in cast iron for the ship industry and the railroad. With the business having crashed with the market in 1929, its doors remained closed until 2013, when Bruno Monnier of Culturespaces saw in the foundry the possibility for a new venue to promote art (and, to be fair, a cash-making enterprise). But this was not the first such repurposing of an industrial building into a repository of art. A Paris train station became the Musée d'Orsay, and a concrete shipping depot on the Seine was transformed into the Cité de la Mode et du Design (Museum of Fashion and Design), among others.

My first visit to L'Atelier des Lumières came shortly after it opened in 2018, when my friends Chantal and Élisabeth invited me to a breathtaking exhibit of Gustav Klimt's works. That one remains my favorite, but my assessment probably stems partly from the fact that the concept was so new and mesmerizing to me. From the moment we entered the Klimt exhibit, we were surrounded by the grandiose music of Wagner, Strauss, Beethoven, and Mahler in succession. The gilded patchwork of elongated women's bodies, a signature style of Klimt's, expanded all around us. Tall, lanky women unfolded above us, below us, around us, with their breasts and abdomens most apparently exposed. Luminescent walls re-created a fantastical version of turn-of-the-century Vienna. A parade of white parasols, diaphanous dresses, trees made of golden swirls, and statuesque Greek figures ensued—a symphony of movement and light.

The next show I saw at L'Atelier des Lumières was for the works of Van Gogh, whose mental fluctuations were reflected in the play of silence and sound, light and darkness, movement and stillness. *Starry Night* swirled into being. Flying cicadas (reminiscent of Van Gogh's time in the South of France, including his stay at a mental sanatorium in Saint Rémy de Provence) dotted the walls and ceiling of the atelier. Japanese-inspired almond blossoms drifted across the sky, and all those in attendance seemed stunned (insofar as you could see them moving in the darkened space).

One art critic complained that, in the Studio of Light, you don't see a chronological exposition of the artist's oeuvre, with explanations for each work, as you do in a museum. In the Atelier des Lumières, you miss the contextualization of the works, the complaint goes. But those comments eclipse the artistry of the form itself: it is a digital reconstruction, replete with movement, light, color, angles, exposure, and sound. The idea is experimental and experiential: How can you immerse yourself in a work of art?

That is exactly what I did on my last trip to the exhibit: I wanted to see if I could gain access to the universe of Salvador Dalí more fully—even if, truth be told, I hadn't been much of a fan. Not far from the front door of the exhibit, you could enter into a room of mirrors in which all the artwork was not only reflected but also projected in a *mise en abyme*—that is, each image had inside of itself its own image, and so on, into infinity. The angular patterns lent themselves well to this exposure.

I walked into the smallish room where several people lined the mirrored walls, sitting on the floor observing. No one remained standing because it was indeed a dizzying spectacle. When I saw that a few children had lain down with knees bent and heads back against the wall, I followed their lead . . . and found that it was a completely different experience seen from that angle! Shortly thereafter, everyone in the room was doing the same thing. It was as if we had all been thinking, *You're not supposed to lie down in a museum, are you?* But this was Dalí, and all bets were off.

In that room, we could see, first, an iridescent Christ figure viewed from below, as in *contre-plongée* (a low-angle shot) in cinema. Then we noticed a Madonna-esque head, quite small, towering from above, her tears rolling toward us. The Christ figure stretched out his arms and began to move his fingers, alternately clenching them and stretching them out. I later learned the intriguing title of the painting on which this video installation was based—*Pietà*, the term used to describe a Christian work of art in which Mary holds the crucified Jesus in her arms. In Dalí's rendition, the Christ figure appeared to be emerging from a gigantic egg, a recurring image in Dalí's work. In this surrealist context, the egg could reflect Jesus's prenatal environment or suggest the promise of resurrection—or both.

Now a rose with unfolding petals came into view, with Pink Floyd accompanying it, an electric guitar sliding wildly on the strings. The translucent rose was mirrored in infinite regression. Then entered blues, oranges, and purples in geometric shapes, like circles with a bite taken out of them. An elephant walked across the wall on spider's legs—though nothing could surprise us at this point. Another bright image broke into floating leaves, psychedelically reflected on the floor, the walls, the ceiling. A tiger opened its mouth wide, as if to roar, and out of its mouth flew another tiger—Dalí's heaven and hell, all rolled into one. Simultaneously arresting and strangely beautiful.

The foundry that once made cast iron now cast light on art.

4

Finding Art Everywhere

Gaze, object, symbol, the {Eiffel} Tower is everything that viewers imagine it to be, and this everything is infinite. A spectacle that is looked at and that looks out, irreplaceable and useless, both familiar world and heroic symbol, witness to a century and always renewed, an inimitable monument that is constantly reproduced, it is a pure sign, open to all times, all images, all meanings—an unstoppable metaphor. Through the Tower, viewers exercise the great power of the imagination, which is freedom. No other history, however somber, could ever take that away from them.

—Roland Barthes

It seems that everywhere you turn in Paris, there is art—architectural masterpieces, statues, sculptures, outdoor exhibits, and more—and the same can be said of many other French cities. While the ideas of timelessness and endurance characterize some forms of art, ephemerality, transience, and fleetingness are also integral to the joy of art.

Take as an example the designed-to-be-temporary Eiffel Tower. When the architect Gustav Eiffel had the edifice constructed for the 1889 Exposition Universelle, no one—not even Gustav Eiffel himself—imagined it would figure prominently over a hundred years later on backpacks, dish towels, and key chains across the world. Yet, even though its tower has remained basically the same, the monument has undergone important changes. It was the tallest structure in the world until 1930, after which international cities vied—and continue to vie—with one another to build taller and taller ones. The tower's original elevators were dismantled and replaced as early as 1910, and the newer elevators have seen major renovations and replacements since then. The monument is systematically repainted every seven years, and its color has varied since its inception, with subtle tints of brown, yellow, and red.

The Eiffel Tower continues to fascinate with its multiple meanings—it stands in as a metonymy for Frenchness and elegance. It has no earthly purpose other than to be there for the enjoyment of all—and that is precisely the point. It was never meant to house meetings or religious services or important artifacts. Whatever you think of it, you must admit that nothing in the world looks quite like it. Nothing seems to be suggesting quite so convincingly, *Come to my unique city. Immerse yourself.*

Imagine this: In an Yves Saint Laurent advertisement that appeared in *Le Monde*, a lanky model's elongated legs echo the curving form of the Eiffel Tower. Her open coat and windswept hair suggest a kind of detached coolness that only Paris (and Yves Saint Laurent) can offer. Luxury is connoted in the gold buckle on the model's four-inch heels. Her leather bodice extends enticingly from between her legs to below breasts that are, however, obscured from the viewer by the coat. The image telegraphs sexiness, as if to conflate sex, the Eiffel Tower, and the brand Yves Saint Laurent. In viewing this ad, anticapitalists might identify the selling of the landmark, the clothing, and the woman's body encapsulated in one ad. Photography buffs might see the stunning angles and the subtly executed lighting. Parisians might see, well, a typical advertisement in France: a striking and sensuous image. And virtually all viewers probably want to be there, beneath the Eiffel Tower, with this elongated beauty. Now.

To celebrate the year 2000, the city of Paris decided to create a light show for the tower that now runs for five minutes on the hour, every hour, from sunset until midnight. During these times, the tower seems to me to become a giant, attenuated, sparkling camel that dances as its twenty thousand gold and white lights flashed off and on in succession. The light show was meant to be temporary, but the public eventually demanded that it be kept—as was the case for the Eiffel Tower itself more than a century before. Each night, as an emblem of both the ephemeral and the eternal, the scintillating camel begins dancing anew, a sensuous delight for viewers everywhere. Whether you are passing by on foot, riding in a bus or aboveground on the métro, or staring out a bedroom window, this sparkling addendum to the day will remind you that, yes, you are alive.

Another at once changing and enduring architectural landmark in Paris is generally much more prized by the French: Notre Dame Cathedral. All roads in France lead to Notre Dame . . . in the sense that distances in France are measured as radiating outward from an eight-pointed star on the esplanade in front of the cathedral, called Point Zéro.

Construction of Notre Dame began in 1163, and the cathedral still reigns over Île de la Cité today (at least most of it does, even as it is being rebuilt). But even before the devastating fire of 2019, Notre Dame had undergone numerous changes that those who clamor for its "identical" reconstruction often ignore, notably, a massive overhaul in the nineteenth century following Victor Hugo's plea for the cathedral's restoration; Eugène Viollet-le-Duc's neo-Gothic spire, added in 1859; and new copper alloy bells, installed in 2013. Thus, the "original" spire has been in place for less than a fourth of the cathedral's existence.

After the fire, architects from all over the planet proposed designs for a new roof for Notre Dame, including several plans with rooftop gardens; daring spires made of metal, glass, or stained glass; and even a swimming pool. Nonetheless, the perception of continuity and tradition won out, in this instance, over creativity and change. Even the most postmodern of architects, Jean Nouvel, was delighted with the government's decision, following the recommendation of the National Heritage and Architecture Commission, to reconstruct the edifice *à l'identique*, or as close as possible to its form just before the fire. Like an artistic Rock of Gibraltar, Notre Dame will rise again, exuding beauty and reassurance to all who pass.

ART MATTERS

The first time I went to the Metropolitan Museum of Art in New York, I stood in the lobby staring dizzily at the map, having no clue where to begin. The museum houses more than 2 million works of art in 2.2 million square feet. While I was pondering my choices, two sprightly middle-aged women walked up next to me and glanced briefly at the map. One turned to the other and said, "Well, as long as we're here, we might as well see it all." And off they went. This phrase has become a humorous shorthand in my family for a wildly enthusiastic, albeit unrealistic, plan—as is often the American way.

A French bus driver once told me that his least favorite job ever was driving a group of tourists who had only one day to spend in Paris before leaving for Provence the next morning. They went straight to the Eiffel Tower for a fifteen-minute stop at the top of the Trocadéro overlook for photos, then along the Seine past the Tuileries Gardens and to the Louvre. This stop was slightly more leisurely, because the tourists had an hour to elbow their way through the crowds to catch a glimpse of the computer screen–size *Mona Lisa*, take a few selfies, and return to the bus for more breathless sightseeing. *As long as we're here . . .*

These are extreme examples, to be sure, but they suggest the intimate relationship between experiencing art and the passage of time. If you are invited to view art all around you—a statue in a Parisian park, a glass-encased exhibit in the métro, immense photographs on the fence around the Luxembourg Gardens, a war memorial in a village square, a colorful mural on a low-rent tenement—then your sense of observation becomes heightened. Like a flâneur (a wanderer without a destination, an observing explorer), you can amble down the street, taking it all in. Baudelaire fashioned the flâneur as the archetype of the (wealthy male) urban modernist, but we postmodern flâneurs— and *flâneuses*—of all backgrounds can appropriate the term as we like. Walking is my absolute favorite thing to do in Paris, and I will choose a distant métro station rather than a close one if it allows me to avoid changing lines or if the walk is in itself pleasurable. In addition to people-watching as you walk, you can also find some form of public art at every turn.

Given the wealth of artistic manifestations in France, it

comes as little surprise to learn that the French government has been supporting artists since 1515, when François I became the first Renaissance king. His subsidizing of art, music, and literature began a long tradition of state-supported arts.

Art historians concerned with cultural appropriation sometimes cite the obvious example of the *Mona Lisa*, which, having been painted by Leonardo da Vinci, should be returned to what is now Italy, right? . . . Not exactly, as it turns out. At François's invitation, Leonardo moved from the Vatican Palace to Amboise in 1516 to become "The King's First Painter, Engineer and Architect." Before Leonardo's death in 1519, the *Mona Lisa* was among the gifts the painter offered the king. The privileging of art as an inextricable part of French life as it unfolds can be seen today in Leonardo's reconstructed studio in the captivating Château du Clos Lucé, in Amboise. In the sixteenth century, as today, art provided viewers with beauty, an invitation to reflect, or both.

François I's support of the arts has continued in some form throughout the centuries and into the present day. Following the first wave of the coronavirus pandemic, the French minister of culture announced a "massive restart" program for the arts. The government devoted thirty million euros to visual arts, music, live performance, writing, design, and other artistic pursuits, with priority given to young artists just finishing their training and entering the professional world. According to statistics gathered by Artnet News in 2021, France ranks first in the world in per capita Covid-19 recovery funds devoted to the arts, almost three times the amount allotted for the same purpose in the United States. And what a good investment it is! Art, the "gift that keeps on giving," enlivens streets, public buildings, and parks. It invites us into museums, sculpture gardens, concert halls, and city squares, bringing people together for a shared experience. It inspires us, makes us think, brings us joy.

SCULPTURE AND SENSUALITY

Near the fountains in the Jardins du Trocadéro (Trocadero Gardens), with the Eiffel Tower spiking the clouds in the background, stands a group of statues called *La Joie de vivre*, created by Léon-Ernest Drivier for the International Exposition of Art and Technology in 1937. Art historians might notice vestiges of the iconic sculptor Auguste Rodin, in whose workshop Drivier first trained. Or they might point out the block stone carving or signs of Drivier's transition from a romantic to a neoclassical sculptor. But what do the rest of us see? How is "the joy of living" depicted?

None of the figures is wearing clothes, save for the occasional drape hanging from a waist—and we quickly understand that the human body is at the center of the enterprise. A first look gives the impression of movement: on the eastern side of the cluster, a woman plays the violin, and a man and woman turn toward each other. Is the woman reaching for the man's hair? (Her hand is obscured behind his head.) Is the man's open hand reaching to touch her? It would seem so. There is definitely some understated romantic electricity going on. On the western side, a nude woman rides a horse, and a figure behind her throws her head backward and looks to the sky. In the southwestern corner, a child avidly draws a piece of fruit (an apple?) to her lips. If the child could be construed as Eve, we might surmise that the Fall gave rise to "joie de vivre"—perhaps a subliminal association.

As if to stage all the senses, the forms suggest the sound of the violin, the aroma and taste of the fruit, the tactile encounter of the rider's thighs squeezing the horse, and the sight of the sky as one woman gazes upward. Humans and animals harmoniously coexist: a goat sits peacefully, nestled between a child and a woman, and the horse has obligingly kneeled so that the rider's foot touches the ground. The most visually stunning connection between human and animal lies in the juxtaposition of the almost-identical swirls of the woman's hair and the horse's tail, highlighting their commonality. This block of statues, aptly named *La Joie de vivre,* celebrates humans, animals, music, movement, and conviviality in the natural world—in the midst of the bustle of Paris.

When I was a student at Berkeley, I formed a secret bond with Pygmalion, because I, too, fell in love with a statue—the difference being that the statue was not Galatea; nor did I sculpt it myself. My statue was tucked away in a cluster of trees by Strawberry Creek, which ran through the campus, and almost no one ever went there. Created by the French sculptor Aristide Maillol in 1922, that statue was my refuge from stacks of books to be read and piles of papers to be graded. It was called *La Douleur* (*Pain*, or *Sorrow*), but, to me, the voluminous oversized woman resting her head on her hand exuded strength and reassurance. I would sit in her lap, surrounded by her force, listening to the rippling murmurs of the creek for just a few minutes. Recharged, I could then climb down and be on my way.

When I was on the verge of moving from Berkeley at the end of my studies, I dropped by the statue to say farewell, thinking that I would probably never see her again; she had been my bronze rock. A few years later, walking in the Jardin

du Carrousel, near the Louvre, I stopped with a jolt. There she was! *La Douleur!* My statue! I don't know why it hadn't occurred to me that there might be copies of her elsewhere, as several sculptures were often made from the same mold or in multiple sizes—as with the Statue of Liberty in New York City, in the Jardin du Luxembourg, and near the Pont de Grenelle in Paris.

I later learned that Maillol's *La Douleur* also sits atop a war memorial in the town of Céret, not far from the Spanish border, offering solace to anyone who desires it, but she does not thrive on attention. In the Jardin du Carrousel, she sits among the hedges, with tourists walking by, eating their ice-cream cones and ignoring this unparalleled work of art and humanity. Her

California avatar has now been taken from its lush natural land-scape of Strawberry Creek to the Berkeley Art Museum, where she is surrounded by concrete. But each time I go to Paris, I reconnect with her in the garden near the Louvre, and each time I do, I derive hope from the strength of her *douleur*.

Two other French sculptors have produced similarly power-ful and sensuous works, bringing inspiration to art enthusiasts and passersby alike: Auguste Rodin and Camille Claudel, both of whom portrayed passion in clay, marble, and bronze. The Musée Rodin is the most magical in all of Paris, with its sumptuous gardens surrounding a converted mansion with creaky parquet floors. Outside, you can find Rodin's mammoth and moving *Les Bourgeois de Calais* (*The Burghers of Calais*), a collection of bronze statues depicting the six town leaders who, during the siege of the city by Edward III's army in 1346, agreed to sacrifice themselves so that the rest of the populace could be spared. At the urging of the English queen consort Philippa of Hainault, when the six Burghers emerged from the besieged city wearing nooses (as instructed), Edward spared their lives as well.

Today their likenesses stand in the garden and in history as symbols of heroic sacrifice and courage. The town of Calais had requested a monument depicting the Burghers as victorious heroes. Instead, Rodin crafted the figures in all their humanity: suffering and resigned to death. The sculptor was honoring a different form of heroism not frequently celebrated in war memorials. Though larger than life, the bodies are so perfectly sculpted that you can imagine them walking through the garden that is home to this work. One of them is hunched over, cradling his head in his hands. In observing Rodin's "studies" (statues made in preparation for the final work), we see that he first sculpted the men nude so that the musculature would be precise in the different poses. In the ultimate version, the Burghers' clothes are in tatters, allowing viewers to catch glimpses of their muscled arms and legs as they journey toward what they thought was certain death.

Also in the museum's gardens, Rodin's iconic *Le Penseur* (*The Thinker*) sits high on a pedestal. Even if you have seen multiple photos of this masterpiece, the statue still comes as a surprise in real life. The Thinker's massive form seems to exude two apparently contradictory ideas: the primacy of the body and the primacy of the intellect—the captivating depiction of a body in thought. What would Descartes have said?

Camille Claudel, Rodin's acolyte and lover—who, many say, surpassed him in her artistic finesse—was also fascinated by bodies and movement, dancers and lovers. When her works are compared with Rodin's, Claudel's material sensuality becomes magnified, enhanced. A room is reserved for her works in the Musée Rodin, and in 2017, a museum devoted exclusively to her art opened in her childhood home of Nogent-sur-Seine. In the nineteenth century, some of her work was deemed too sensual to have been sculpted by a "lady," but many people today find her statues, particularly the marble *Vertumne et Pomone*, to be achingly beautiful.

In Camille Claudel's sculptures, bodies seem to fuse with nature, as in the terra-cotta *Young Girl with a Sheaf*, in which the Girl's rust-hued back seems to morph into the wheat, and in the famous *Waltz*, where the dancing woman's skirt flows into bronze-like lava. We are invited to join in, to be transported into nature, and to dance as the sculptures come alive.

DEPICTING JOY

Virtually every historical period in French painting has in some way foregrounded the good life *à la française* as crystalized in the plenitude of a particular moment. Jean-Baptiste Greuze, known for sensitively capturing the hardships of the poor in eighteenth-century France, paints a moving portrait of a young

peasant girl winding wool. The viewer's eye is soon drawn to the side of the painting, where a cat plays with yarn the girl is about to knit. Just as the surrealists promulgated the concept of "found objects" they transformed into art, so Greuze creates a "found moment" of quiet joy.

Such moments can be glimpsed in the least expected places: Eugène Delacroix, famous for his dramatic portrayals (revolutions, wild tigers, swordsmen on bucking horses), also painted luminous sailboats at sunset in Dieppe and calm and luxuriant gardens, inviting viewers to step into these stunning, true-to-life landscapes. Similarly, Édouard Manet's *Le Déjeuner sur l'herbe* (*The Luncheon on the Grass*), while challenging artistic conventions, depicts a lovely picnic in the countryside.

The nude woman, a recurring image in artistic works, had always looked demurely down or into the distance. Here,

however, she contradicts expectations by staring directly at the viewer—the reverse gaze becomes part of the painting's originality. Why are the women illuminated with "studio light" and nude or lightly dressed, whereas the men are comparatively in shadow and fully dressed in dark clothing? Why are the three characters in the foreground not engaged in conversation with one another? Do the men imagine the nude woman to be simply a model for a painting? Art historians have advanced various theories on all these questions, but for our purposes, let's examine one element that stands out: In the end, this daring and controversial work by the founder of modernism portrays a luncheon, replete with fruit and bread spilling temptingly out of a basket. What better way to start an artistic revolution than through an enticing picnic in the grass?

Another creator of sumptuous scenes, Henri Matisse, fashioned sculpted bodies lying in beautiful poses, dancing, and making music. His painting *Le Bonheur de vivre* (*The Joy of Life*), depicts insouciant bodies basking in the sun, stretching, dancing, embracing. While the setting was probably inspired by a bucolic landscape, it has an abstract, otherworldly aspect to it. The spatial distortions and blasts of bright color reminiscent of early modernists met with some disdain in the art world around the turn of the twentieth century, but Matisse's scene of unencumbered happiness has become among the most celebrated paintings in modernist art.

These French artists not only reproduce joy; they also create it, re-create it, and "pay it forward."

STREET SPIRIT

Countless French artists' renderings of joie de vivre can be found throughout the magnificent museums of France, but you can also find them in the street. My friend Eve—the director of a *resto du coeur* (soup kitchen) and a fast friend since we were both nineteen—is a devoted fan of spunky present-day street art. (Although *arts urbains* is the official name for it, seemingly everyone, insisting on the plurality of the art form, says, "St*rr*eet art," with French *r*'s.) One day, Eve and I decided to visit the growing number of neighborhoods in Paris where murals have sprouted up on the sides of buildings and along retaining walls. It turns out that this is a continually evolving and potentially never-ending endeavor.

Some areas of Paris are particularly rich in street art, like the 13th arrondissement, home to a large shopping center, the city's "Chinatown," and a campus of the University of Paris known as Grands Moulins (Great Mills) because, to house its classrooms, the university repurposed industrial flour mills constructed during World War I—and yes, I really have participated in seminars in a former flour mill. Walking down the boulevard Vincent Auriol, which has become an open-air museum, you can enjoy no fewer than twenty-six giant murals by both French and international artists. Particularly striking is the mural *Liberté, égalité, fraternité*, by Shepard Fairey, painted in honor of the victims of the terrorist attack on the Bataclan theater in November 2015. Also in the 13th is the *Chat bleu*, a blue cat bathed in moonlight, by the French artist "C215"; and also the skeleton of a cat on its hind legs reaching the height of the building, by the Belgian artist Roa, who has said she was inspired by the dinosaur skeletons in Paris's National History Museum.

Another of my favorite areas for street art is Les Halles (the former site of the largest fresh-food market in Paris, which was replaced in the 1960s by an underground shopping mall and a large park at street level). First, you go up the rue Montorgueil, past the piles of perfect peas and pears and peaches, past the fish displayed on ice, past the tempting *boulangeries* and *pâtisseries*, past a beautiful young woman offering you a small sample of pizza so that you'll dine at her pizzeria, past cafés with tiny tables and handsome youths sipping Apérol spritzes, and past a lone scooter driver trying not very successfully to thread his way through the pedestrian crowd. And there, at the top of that street, stands a four-story wall covered by what at first appears to be an image of a very typical yellow-and-blue Tintin cartoon, perfectly executed. But, wait—Captain Haddock isn't simply leaning over Tintin; the two are kissing! And every time you walk by, they're still making out. It has become one of the most celebrated must-sees for LGBTQ+ visitors to Paris.

Laurent, a street artist, gives informal tours of another area rich in street art: Montmartre. He points out that, for many street artists, these "deposits" on walls and fences and windows are proof of their existence . . . much like graffiti and, centuries before that, the celebrated cave paintings at Lascaux. One artist has even made this claim his signature, with white rectangular stickers posted all over Paris: *J'EXISTE*. Laurent showed us several examples of the work of Miss.Tic, one of the rare famous woman street artists. Her trademark work is stencils of sexy dark-haired women with a subversive slogan on the side, such as *De mes frasques je fais des fresques* ("I make murals from my escapades/transgressions," with a play on words with *frasque/fresque*) and *La solitude est la rançon de la lucidité* (Solitude is the price paid for lucidity). Another woman artist who goes by the name "Intra Larue" began her exploration by making plaster models of her own breasts, just for fun. Then she decided to make them in fantastic colors and designs and attach them to gray walls around Paris, to bring a bit of humanity to them and break some taboos while making a statement in favor of freedom. There are now some five hundred of these "busts" on Parisian walls, though many are hidden behind vines and branches, so they'll be less likely to be removed. Finally, OJA, another woman artist represented throughout the capital, posts portraits of women stars, in her words, both sacralizing and de-sacralizing them. A portrait of Catherine Deneuve includes the slogan (in French) I AM NOT A MONUMENT, and an image of singer Patricia Kaas is accompanied by GET ME OUT OF THE FRAME. At the same time, OJA doesn't intend for her art to be taken so seriously: "Be free," she writes, "have fun, and make Art into the art of living"—which pretty much sums up the raison d'être of street art.

Like Intra Larue with her five hundred breasts glued to walls around Paris, many other street artists have adopted a theme and run with it. Perhaps the first "serialized" street art was created by "Invader," who literally invades spaces with his ceramic tile mosaics ("Rubikcubism") reminiscent of the pioneering video game *Space Invaders*. Finding Invader's tiles has now become a game in the form of the mobile app Flash Invaders, which allows you to locate his designs in a kind of scavenger hunt, principally in Paris, but also all over Europe and in a few locations in Asia, Southeast Asia, the Middle East, North America, and Central America. A graduate of the famed École des Beaux Arts in Paris, the anonymous Invader eschewed the traditional art world to create a new movement of "art for all."

Street art took on a more personal note for me the day Eve and I met an artist who goes by the name "Marko 93," a known figure in the street art circles of northern Paris. I had assumed that the number in his moniker was the year of his birth, but he told us that it instead represented his home, Saint Denis, in postal code 93, the most diverse suburb of Paris, as we saw in Inès Reg's stand-up sketch. (Then it dawned on me: the name for the cocktail French 75, made with sparkling wine, gin, a twist of lemon, and simple syrup, was probably taken from Paris's postal code! But I was wrong on that front, too. The name comes from the seventy-five-millimeter field gun used by the French in World War II. So much for my sleuth-ing abilities.)

Eve and I met Marko 93 on the rue Oberkampf, in the 11th arrondissement, where the wall of a multi-story building has become a revolving canvas for street art. The unassuming café next to it invites artists to submit designs, works are chosen and executed, and each mural is allowed to remain on the wall for two weeks. One day, as we rounded the corner en route to the café, Eve and I stopped in our tracks, stunned by the sight in front of us. Marko 93 was perched high on scaffolding, making the final, sweeping touches to his mural with a can of spray paint. With intent blue eyes, a gigantic tiger stared at us from about twenty-five feet above the ground, its fangs exposed. Its white whiskers spiked outward from its face like lightning against a background of indigo sky. Extending like wild pointillist dots to the edges of the building, the tiger's gold-tufted fur exuded force and beauty. From the bottom of its fangs, blood dripped down the wall toward Marko 93's signature, and white splotches on its fur also streaked downward, denoting movement. Every marking on the tiger's forehead was perfectly formed.

In awe, we settled at a table without taking our eyes off the mural. As the manager of the café walked by, Eve blurted out, "This masterpiece can stay up only two weeks before it's painted over? But this one is so gorgeous—surely you could make an exception? Only two weeks?"

Before the manager could reply, a woman with flowing red hair standing nearby, looking for all the world as though she had just stepped out of a pre-Raphaelite painting, smiled know-ingly and interjected, "But that's the *point*. Street art, like life, is ephemeral. It's beautiful, and then it's gone, only to be replaced by something else. That's what it's all about."

The manager seemed relieved that somebody else was willing to explain the situation, absolving him of the repetitive task.

"Okay for the idea," Eve replied, "but, really? Only two weeks?!"

By this time, other patrons were throwing in their two cents:

"Oh yes, totally—the mural should stay longer!"

"But that would throw off the schedule."

"Yes, but what's more important, schedules or art?"

"And also, the concept is precisely that street art is temporary."

"Well, yes, but can't it still be temporary and be there for more than two weeks?"

"But other artists are waiting their turn!"

And on went the discussion. Meanwhile, we noticed that Marko 93 had climbed down from the scaffolding, so we went over to talk with him while he took a cigarette break. After metaphorically falling at his feet, we chatted a bit about his art and his background.

Marko 93 grew up making graffiti art, like many budding artists, but he eventually turned to larger, more pictorial pursuits. In addition to murals, he also does "light painting" in photography, a technique most notably used by surrealist artist Man Ray in the 1930s. Marko 93 also invented his own version of "calligraffiti," an experimental art that incorporates graffiti-like forms from several linguistic traditions, including Arabic and Asian languages.

We thanked him for his impressive work. To our surprise,

he gave each of us a poster of one of his more permanent tiger murals in Paris. Eve was elated that there were others of Marko's tigers to add to our long list of street art to visit, and I was delighted at the idea that one of his big cats would be featured on the wall of my office. In fact, I am so devoted to that poster that I position it directly behind me in Zoom calls, and Marko 93's once-ephemeral tiger fiercely lives on.

AT THE MOVIES

Je ne veux pas montrer, mais donner l'envie de voir.
(I don't want to show, but to give the desire to see.)
—Agnès Varda

Motion pictures were born in La Ciotat, a smallish port city on the French Mediterranean coast, when, in 1895, the aptly named Louis Lumière held a showing at a local theater, the Eden. Because Louis and his brother had long been known for their photographic experimentation, the townspeople came expecting to see something like a slide show. Instead, the images on the wall were moving!

The first reaction in the crowd was panic. A life-size train was coming toward them! They ran toward the exits in terror. But fear soon morphed into fascination and amusement. This apocryphal story has been called the "founding myth of cinema," but the locals swear by it. By all accounts, it was the first time an audience shared the communal experience of watching pictures move. Since then, French filmmakers have brought audiences joy—as well as consternation, sympathy, compassion, anger, love, indifference, and much food for thought.

Joie de vivre makes an appearance in so many French films that it would be impossible to do justice to them all here. While the New Wave, arguably the most celebrated period of French cinema to date, was notably not characterized by its upbeat films, one of the filmmakers of that historical moment does distinguish herself as a creator of joy: the indefatigable Agnès Varda. Varda died in 2019 at age ninety, and her last film and final celebration of life, *Varda by Agnès*, appeared just months before her death.

As a writer in *Vogue* recently proclaimed, "There are two kinds of people in the world: those who love the director Agnès Varda and those who don't yet know her work." *Cléo from 5 to 7* (1962) was Varda's first successful film. Her pioneering style in this film includes winking "citations" from the work of other filmmakers; a brief tribute to silent burlesque film; inserts (a ticking clock); and symbols (a broken mirror and masks indicating the roles that women play). What has always intrigued me about *Cléo from 5 to 7* is that it is less the story of a woman awaiting medical tests that will determine her fate than it is a story *behind* a story. A few anecdotes about how the film was made remind us of Varda's precise, virtuoso filmmaking but especially of her commitment to humanizing her subjects.

With no digital corrections possible in 1960s editing rooms, viewers of this film today might be amazed to realize that all the filming involving clocks on city streets (of which there are several) had to reflect some precise time between five and seven; and if the weather was radically different from the previous day's filming, the actors and crew would have to wait for another day, on an extremely limited film budget.

Varda's heightened focus on human emotion comes through in her use of mirrors, of fantasy, and of close-ups. At the end of the film, as the camera retreats in a back zoom (traveling) shot,

Cléo and a soldier named Antoine walk away from the hospital together with enigmatic yet hopeful expressions. Cléo says, *"Il me semble que je suis heureuse"* (It seems to me that I'm happy). Varda filmed the most perfect shot of the characters in a close-up and pronounced the work complete. But after the film had wrapped, she saw in the rushes (the unedited footage) that the tracks of the dolly on which the camera had been riding were visible in the background, just above the heads of Cléo and Antoine. The film's budget was already stretched, but Varda had to call back the entire crew and refilm that final scene several times to get the right ending. When she returned to the rushes, however, none of the new scenes reproduced the magic of the facial expressions she had captured with that first take. In this case, she decided to privilege emotion over technique.

When I first saw the film, I didn't even notice the tracks above the two lovers' heads, nor did any of my students. Instead, viewers are intensely focused on the human characters—as was Varda herself.

The humanity in French films is often linked to humor, which ranges from slapstick to surreal to intellectual, in both its traditional and multicultural forms. Despite their sophistication (or perhaps as an antidote to that sophistication), the French sometimes astound me by their love of silly and slapstick humor. They adore comedies and laugh endlessly at the jokes, both during the film and in later conversations referring to them. The cult film *Les Visiteurs* is a case in point. In this wildly popular comedy from the 1990s—it repeatedly appears on lists of the funniest French movies of all time—two medieval men (one of whom is played by Jean Reno) time-travel to the twentieth century, with all the attendant misunderstandings one can imagine. Unlike Swift's *Gulliver's Travels* or Montesquieu's *Persian*

Letters, in which an outsider offers poignant and critical perspectives on his society, here the medieval visitors simply produce gag after gag—like washing their hands in a toilet bowl and setting an umbrella on fire while attempting to use it to roast a leg of lamb. The list of asinine shenanigans is long. One of the most famous scenes involves Jacquouille la Fripouille (Jackal the Rascal), who turns on a light switch in a dark room and, amazed, proclaims, *"Jour!"* (Day!), and when he turns it off, *"Nuit!"* (Night!), and he continues to revel in his newfound powers: *"Jour! Nuit! Jour! Nuit! . . ."* I cannot count the number of times I have heard someone in France puckishly say *"Jour!"* or *"Nuit!"* in turning on or off a light switch, with all the onlookers clearly in on the joke. On another level, however, the numerous references to medieval France remind viewers of their shared history in the country of knights-errant and French Arthurian legends.

There is almost always something under the surface of the silliness, something more thought-provoking and interesting. Among the most highly rated titles by the French public is *Le Dîner des cons* (remade in the United States as *Dinner for Schmucks*). It took me years to decide to see this film, despite rave reviews, because of its questionable title. *Con* is a vulgar term for the most female of body parts, but it now signifies someone stupid or idiotic, which did not strike me as a promising premise.

In the film, the character Pierre Brochard, a wealthy editor, and a few of his friends arrange to host dinners each week to see who can invite the dimmest dimwit. One such guest, a boomerang collector who lectures unsuspecting victims about the history and variety of boomerangs, has already been invited to that week's dinner, and Pierre is desperate to find a better *con*. His friend alerts him to a short, rotund, homely fellow who works as a clerk in the finance ministry; the man makes scale models with matchsticks to help him forget that his wife ran off with his good friend two years before. Pierre is convinced that he has found a winner.

As masterfully played by Jacques Villeret, the last of the *cons* ends up bungling everything he touches. However, the "dumbest" is also the kindest—generous, forgiving, and slow to judge. True to French form, tax fraud is involved (*recel des biens*), and several of the characters are engaged in extramarital affairs, but in the end, even amid sometimes cruel humor, goodness trumps cunning—at least in the viewers' eyes.

Many other French comedies figuring among the classics take on difficult subjects from a humorous angle, including *La Grande Vadrouille* (literally "The Big Jaunt," but translated for English viewers as *Don't Look Now—We're Being Shot At!*), in which French and British soldiers wend their way through the occupied zone during World War II. A similarly grim premise undergirds *Le Père Noël est une ordure* (Santa Claus Is a Stinker), set in the office of a suicide helpline, where a despondent Santa Claus is in need of aid. Neither of these situations sounds the least bit funny, and that's the point, when one amusing thing after the other unfolds. *Bienvenue chez les Ch'tis* (Welcome to the Sticks), by Dany Boon, warmheartedly makes fun of the sparsely populated north of France and, at the same time, embraces its good qualities, chiding those who deride northerners. More recent comedies, such as *Qu'est-ce qu'on a fait au Bon Dieu* (literally, "What Have We Done to God?," but officially, "Serial [Bad] Weddings"), along with its sequel, takes on, in daringly humorous ways, the conundrums of racism and religious prejudice.

The French love to laugh. And while we outsiders don't always share in their hilarity, we can appreciate their reveling in it.

LONG LIVE MUSIC

While writing a poem about not writing a poem about Paris, Gaël Faye makes an excellent point, one that is illustrated implicitly throughout his song "Paris métèque": Paris is Paris not in spite of, but *because of* its immigrants. Roughly 12 percent of French residents are immigrants, and that figure accounts only for first-generation immigrants. It is exciting to hear West African rhythms and *rai* (a type of Algerian fusion pop music) that have been increasingly incorporated in the songs of French vocal artists. While many in these groups justifiably insist on maintaining their separate cultural identities and practices, they have also enriched French musical culture immeasurably.

Although it is not directly linked to French colonialism, American jazz (itself a hybrid of African, Afro-Cuban, and American influences) has also affected French musical traditions. Jazz was imported with great success during and following World War I. Historians have shown that while it was first regarded by the French as American or Black music, it became fully integrated into French entertainment culture by the end of the 1920s. There were, however, a few staunch resisters—like Georges Duhamel, whose 1931 diatribe was translated as *America the Menace*. Jazz remains perennially in fashion in France, with evolutions from bebop to improv to Brazilian to a French version of *jazz manouche* (with an eastern European flavor, questionably translated as "gypsy jazz").

For Lucie Buathier, music coordinator of the Paris Jazz Club, a clearinghouse for promoting and democratizing jazz, "Jazz is very much linked to France, and France is linked to jazz." There are more than seventy-five jazz clubs in Paris, with many other venues also featuring jazz on a regular basis. While New Orleans, New York, Montreal, and Copenhagen all claim to be the jazz capital of the world, Paris must not be far behind.

Music accompanies virtually every joyous occasion in France, and in some cases, it is the very *reason* for the celebration. The Fête de la musique (a national celebration of music), instituted in 1982 by the then-minister of culture, Jack Lang, occurs every year on June 21, around the summer solstice. It is the most wide-ranging, egalitarian festival I know of. While the Paris Opera might be producing *Manon Lescaut* and the National Orchestra of France might be playing Rachmaninoff's Symphony No. 2, thousands of musicians of all ages are playing on every street corner, not only in Paris but also in cities, towns, and villages throughout France. Musicians not performing in a formal venue like the terrace of a café or in the Jardin du Luxembourg need only claim a tiny piece of real estate on the sidewalk as a performance space. As you walk down the street in the evening and throughout the night of June 21, you hear different kinds of music on every block—guitars, accordions, West African drums, chamber groups, reggae, jazz . . .

When my daughters, Laura and Lise, were aged nine and twelve, all the violin students in their music school, the Schola Cantorum, played in a makeshift orchestra on the rue Saint Jacques. When the Schola opened its doors in 1896, all elementary music classes were free. The school is now famous for counting among its alumni such luminaries as Erik Satie, Cole Porter, and Claire Delbos. Though the building housing it is an antiquated English Benedictine convent with peeling paint and cracking walls, its teachers remain among the best in Paris—if you can make beautiful music, who cares about the décor? The child string players certainly didn't notice the dilapidated building as they attracted crowds with their reasonably well-played Boccherini Minuet from *Suzuki Violin Book 2*. Well, okay, so most in the crowd were proud parents, but passersby also stopped on their way to hear other street musicians.

The Fête de la musique recalls the carnivals of the medieval and Renaissance eras. In those times, folk festivals featured a topsy-turvy world in which hierarchies and social status were obliterated or reversed. The Fête de la musique seems to do just that: in the streets of France, for the space of an evening, all are invited to partake, and music of all sorts is welcome.

I happened to be in Tours staying with friends for last year's Fête de la musique, and the downtown was alive with crowds, music, bright balloons of sundry shapes, and food trucks. This scene was thrilling to my friend's five-year-old daughter, who rode on her father's shoulders. Not a seat was to be had in any of the open-air cafés. In a narrow pedestrian street off the central boulevard, a rock band blared tunes from the 1960s, '70s, and '80s, singing the French songs with perfect intonation and the American and English songs with heavy French accents, or else in gibberish—in the sing-alongs, "Saturday night" often comes out as *Sananana*. The street overflowed with people dancing, others straining to see the band, and yet others carefully weaving their way through the crowd to find a missing friend. Meanwhile, in the courtyard of an old convent, an African French evangelical group was singing upbeat gospel songs with the crowd clapping and stomping in time to the beat. On a side street, Latin music reverberated from loudspeakers, and a couple was giving impromptu lessons in what looked like salsa dance, their posteriors facing the crowd. Lines of hip-shakers stood behind them, attempting to imitate the movements by throwing their hips willy-nilly in every direction. This musical paradise—name your poison!—continued through the night.

Some French singers never die, including of course the legendary Édith Piaf, who by all accounts will sing forever. Even living singers who somehow embody the French soul engage an audience of as many as three generations. Francis Cabrel, an unmistakably southern French singer who became wildly popular around 1980, is still producing successful albums and tours today. One of his most adorable qualities is his accent from the area in and around Toulouse, aka La Ville Rose ("the Pink City," named after the color of the terra-cotta bricks used in much of its architecture). Cabrel pronounces the *o* in *Rose* like "uh", as in "ruhz," and pronounces the otherwise silent terminal *e* in the word as many times as he can fit into one sentence. During the coronavirus lockdown—known in French as the *confinement* (a word that Cabrel pronounces in four syllables)—he released one song a day, to the delight of fans.

Of all the artists I have seen play live (from gospel singer Mahalia Jackson when I was a child to the Rolling Stones when I was a student to Lady Gaga more recently), I have never before felt such multigenerational unity as I did during the Cabrel concert at the Olympia, the oldest "music hall" in Paris. That evening, I looked around the auditorium to see a crowd of children, teenagers, and adults, all ranging in age from roughly ten to eighty. When Cabrel began to sing one of his biggest hits from the 1980s, "Je l'aime à mourir" (I love her so much I could die), I was quite sure that only the "oldies" in the audience would be singing along. But no—*everyone* was singing along. I was moved by the jaw-dropping togetherness of that multigenerational, multiracial crowd singing in unison.

The song "Je l'aime à mourir" has taken on many avatars: After occupying the top spot on the charts in France, it became popular in Spain and Latin America as "La quiero a morir." Shakira released a cover of it in French and Spanish. But fantastic parodies of the iconic song have also been produced. My friends and I used to compile lists of alternate, rhyming titles: "Je l'aime à courir/flétrir/pourrir/fou rire" (I love her so much I could run/wilt/rot/die laughing). Scores of parodies circulate on the internet, including "Je l'aide à maigrir" (I'm helping her lose weight) or "Je baise à mourir" (I f*** so much I could die). These reinventions don't have quite the same poetic qualities, but they continue to keep the music alive.

5

Defining Frenchness

To try to assemble the puzzle pieces of the French joie de vivre, it might be helpful to consider what it means to be French. From my very first sojourns in France, of all the examples of French exceptionalism I heard, the most common was that French people were individualistic (implication: not like Americans or Spaniards or Japanese, who all do the same thing). "We all like to do things our own way." This frequently heard statement puzzled me as I looked around: Virtually all the women were wearing scarves, and almost everyone of all genders was wearing black. Everywhere, people were carrying baguettes home, with a missing section on one end in cases where the carrier served as the king's taster for his family. Once, while in a store trying on a skirt, I found that my raincoat was a little too short to cover it. The helpful saleswoman told me that, as for the length of my raincoat, *"Ça ne se fait pas cette année"* (That just isn't done this year)—I wasn't conforming enough to the new norm.

In conversations, I also heard from numerous French people that Americans (present company excepted, of course) were louder, less sophisticated, and less subtle than the French. And almost everyone told me that the reason there were more political parties—and more cheeses!—in France than elsewhere was because French tastes were so divergent and distinct.

It eventually dawned on me that all of us think our culture is more varied than outsiders do. When my husband (of Scottish descent) spent several years in Japan, he was asked repeatedly how we *gaijin* (foreigners) can tell one another apart. I guess it's all about the nuances: The ubiquitous scarves Frenchwomen wear are of varying colors and shapes, and there must be fifty ways to tie them. I love the way the French rapper Casey sums up the question of sartorial conformity. She laughs at the idea that a baseball cap worn backward is stereotypical of a teenager from the *banlieue*, but lawyers wearing suits or writers wearing shirts unbuttoned down a few notches do not imagine themselves to look stereotypical in any way.

We all like to imagine ourselves, as the American rapper will.i.am once termed it, as "architects of our own frequency." But we all inevitably absorb, at least to some extent, the cultural forces around us.

The French define themselves the most clearly, it seems to me, through culture. While the French cultural scene seems continually vibrant, France is not without its curmudgeons who wish for a return to what is perceived as high culture. The French cultural critic Alain Finkielkraut laments that while *grande culture* illuminates, pop culture simply entertains. "A pair of boots is now worth Shakespeare," he complains. But Finkielkraut isn't looking closely enough: *Grande culture* has never been lost. *Au contraire.* Many contemporary singers incorporate or sample classical music, the once-staid Comédie Française now produces plays by both Molière and Marie NDiaye, and the Philharmonie de Paris hosts African pop singers. It is not a question of either/

or, but rather of both/and. The public bandwidth has proven to be wide enough to accommodate all.

High culture and popular culture are only a part of the French cultural landscape, however. Any sense of our own culture is inevitably influenced by where we live, whom we associate with, how we imagine ourselves in community, what character traits we share, what languages we speak, and much more.

Ever since my first stay in France, I have noted things that, for me, define Frenchness—the family, the village, the neighborhood, the French public school, the underdog, the power of debate, and of course (*bien sûr!*), France's defense of its beloved language.

THE FAMILY

La famille occupies a central place in French culture, although its role has inevitably evolved in recent years. It's impossible for me to think of France without evoking my French family and the model it provides. I would say "host family," as the Habigs were not technically related to me, but that term doesn't do justice to our situation.

I became part of the Habig family during my second long stay in France, in Saint Étienne. My French host mother, who became a second mother to me, created a household filled with mirth and *complicité*. When we think of the word *complicity* in English, we imagine conspiracy and plots and collusion, but *complicité* in French most often means "affinity," "a forged bond," "intimacy." When Madame Habig's husband died in his forties of cancer, she was forced to raise six children as a single mother. (All of them have become delightful adults.) She accomplished this feat, I later realized, by several psychological strategies she must have learned or invented along the way.

The first strategy was humor. When one of the children made a pun or told a (usually dumb) joke, Madame Habig sometimes laughed till she cried, laughter that everyone else caught and joined in on—first, by laughing at her laugh and, then, laughing with her. When I first arrived in their home, I thought, *Well, the joke wasn't THAT funny*, but then I began to see the kind of atmosphere my host mother was creating, and as I slid into that world, I, too, began to laugh hysterically, genuinely, at similar jokes.

Second, my host mother was parsimonious with her criticism but lavish with her praise. "Oh, did you see that Bertrand set the table? Thank you, Bertrand! And look! Zef, our poet, is washing the dishes. Everyone is pitching in! Aren't you the best?"

And then there was her famous *salade de riz*, which consisted of rice, tomatoes, olives, and French vinaigrette made with mustard. Sometimes it had hard-boiled eggs on top. I could never figure out why the entire family was so enthusiastic about this plain dish, but years later, once again, it finally struck me. Their *mère poule* (mother hen), having been a middle school teacher earlier in her career, had learned quite a bit about drumming up enthusiasm. Every time rice salad was on the menu for the evening, she would say, in her most excited voice, "Guess what we're having for dinner? . . . *Une salade de riz!*" Never mind that it was simply the cold rice left over from the day before with a few other things thrown in. Seated around the large table, with an immense bowl of *salade de riz*, a little red wine, a little cheese, and a lot of baguette, we whiled away the evening, chatting and laughing.

Petite Mère (an affectionate nickname for "mother") believed so much in creating joy around her that she also made sure everyone was paired up, becoming a matchmaker on more than one occasion. Her concept of happiness was that no matter who you were, you should, if at all possible, have both a partner and a multigenerational family around you . . . so much so that she is partly responsible for my deciding to get married, as unlikely as that may sound.

The first summer I spent with the Habig family, Petite Mère asked me—all this took place in French—"Do you have a long-term boyfriend?"

"Well, I did, but I called it off. Because I think we're too young to get serious—we're only in our early twenties."

"Why? Don't you like him?" she challenged.

"Oh yes, I like him a lot, but I just think it's better to be free at this stage."

"Is something wrong with him?"

"Not at all."

"He's not smart?"

"Oh yes, he is, he's brilliant, but . . ." (This conversation wasn't going anywhere, I was convinced.)

"So, he's not good to you . . ."

"It's not that, for sure. He's one of the kindest people I know."

"Okay, so he's nice, but he's ugly."

"Are you kidding?"

"So . . . ?"

This feels like an interrogation. "So, what?"

"So, who is it you're waiting for?"

I wanted to say "no one," but maybe that wasn't exactly true.

That conversation set me on a course of contemplation that ultimately took me down a very different path—one I'm still on today. And to quote Édith Piaf, *"Je ne regrette rien."* The family route isn't for everyone, but it turned out to be a fortunate one for me, and it was Petite Mère standing at the junction who nudged me in that felicitous direction.

My French family also pointed out my cultural mishaps, of which there were many. When Régis, my youngest host brother, and I left a shop together early in my stay in Saint Étienne, he remarked, "You're not very polite."

"Why do you say that?" I inquired, incredulous. If there was one thing my parents had insisted on, it was to be kind to salespeople, waiters, bank tellers, janitors . . . They are all human beings like us, and they do not exist to help us.

"Well," he replied patiently, "you didn't say *Bonjour, madame* when we entered the shop, and you didn't say *Au revoir, madame* when we left."

"But we were talking with the shopkeeper, and she was quite nice," I retorted.

"Yes, but you didn't say *Bonjour, madame* and you didn't say *Au revoir, madame.*"

Although the use of honorifics like *Madame, Monsieur,* and *Mademoiselle* has recently faded somewhat, you're still considered uncouth if you begin a conversation without saying *Bonjour.* That extra little word seems redundant to us Americans, particularly if we're standing directly in front of someone and we have something to say. Occasionally, I forget this crucial formula and begin a sentence using the extremely polite conditional tense, *Pardon, monsieur, pourriez-vous me dire . . .* (Excuse me, sir, could you please tell me . . .). Just this year, when I asked a white-haired man for information about the schedule as he was waiting at a bus stop, he said firmly, *"BONJOUR,"* correcting me in my apparent arrogance. So, I began again, *"Bonjour, monsieur, pourriez-vous me dire . . ."* and suddenly he relaxed and kindly answered my question. Now my task will be to remember that a conversation with a stranger is like a Boolean domain (a set of precisely two elements, notably {0,1}): With *bonjour* = yes; without *bonjour* = no possible way.

I remember the circle around the fireplace after dinner at the Habigs' country home, passing around *tablettes* of Chocolat Weiss, each of us taking a square, like a cookie shared between two people: You break it in half. Your partner breaks the half in half. You break the fourth in half. He breaks the eighth in half, and so on, until you are trying to split the very last crumb. As the chocolate was passed around, we sang various traditional French songs, like "Aux Marches du palais" (On the steps of the palace) and "Il faut que je m'en aille," whose lyrics speak of joy: "*Buvons encore, une dernière fois, à l'amitié, l'amour, la joie*" (Let's drink one last time to friendship, love, and joy), accompanied by guitars. And we laughed together mirthfully at very bad jokes.

In addition to the celebration of the *salade de riz* and the chocolate bar ritual, making *café au lait* in the mornings was also a happy rite for the Habig clan. Each morning, a big Bialetti espresso maker was filled with finely ground coffee and cold water and placed on a gas burner, with a pan of milk heated on the burner next to it. Meanwhile, we prepared the *tartines* (baguette slices with butter and jam). The espresso maker purportedly made fourteen small cups of espresso, but when eight adults and almost-adults all want big bowls of *café au lait*, just one batch is not sufficient. Only Marie, the youngest of the children, still drank hot chocolate in the mornings. If the milk was heated too long or too quickly, a thick crust formed on the top—and the Habig brothers inevitably fought over it.

"Mine!"

"No, mine!"

Let them argue, I thought, before realizing that it was another of Petite Mère's strategies: Convert the undesirable into the desirable, and everyone is contented with their lot. The same went for the "privilege" of sleeping in the dormitory of the third floor of the old stone country house when we ran out of bedrooms. Today, the country house has been sold, with the Habig family now scattered to the South of France, Paris, Brussels, and Sydney, but even across the globe, the clan remains tight, representing for me the most cherished of France's treasures.

VILLAGE LIFE

The village remains a fundamental element of French identity. Seemingly of fairy tales, French villages are tucked into hillsides, nestled in forests, or chiseled into mountain slopes. Unfortunately, French villages have experienced a steady decline in population since the early 1990s.

One of the many regrettable consequences of the loss of population in France's small villages is the dearth of doctors. Until recently, few young, urban medical students could imagine living like small-town doctors, being called to homes at all hours to attend to births, illnesses, and deaths. In the United States (depending on a given state's regulations), deaths can be certified by doctors, medical examiners, coroners, sheriffs, and others, but only a doctor can declare a death in France. And this declaration is no small matter, as history has confirmed.

Vengeful hearsay and its continuation for centuries held that Catherine de Médicis had destined a poison-laced book for Henri de Navarre, a competitor for the throne of France, but that her son Charles IX first picked up the book and succumbed to its poison. At least that's the story distilled from accounts ranging from sixteenth-century xenophobic rumors—Catherine was resented as an Italian among French royalty—to her maternal role in Alexandre Dumas *père*'s *La Reine Margot* (*Queen Margot*) in 1845. However, Ambroise Paré, Charles IX's royal *chirurgien* (his "surgeon," as doctors then were often called), dutifully declared the king dead and wrote up his autopsy in 1574. The true cause of death was much less scheming and less dramatic: tuberculosis. But it took a doctor to set the record straight.

Today, in a few communes where no doctor is easily available, some families have had to keep their dead relatives at home for hours, sometimes more than a day, until a doctor could travel to certify the death. There is a bit of good news, however: Macron's government has promised to raise the salaries for rural doctors and to give scholarships to medical students who promise a certain number of years of practice in lesser-served areas. Furthermore, following the onset of the Covid-19 pandemic of the early 2020s, some city-dwellers have questioned whether they want to remain in crowded urban areas, locked up in their small apartments, when they could be in the countryside, roaming about freely and taking advantage of the extra space and natural bounty.

Another central question that village life poses is where to buy bread. It is a truth universally acknowledged that the bakery holds a venerated place in French life—so venerated, in fact, that entire literary works have been devoted to it. In Jean Giono's short story "La femme du boulanger" (The Baker's Wife), a village begins to come unraveled when the baker's young wife runs away with a shepherd. The middle-aged baker goes on strike until his wife returns, and the entire village collaborates to ensure her return. Marcel Pagnol (of *My Father's Glory* fame) made a classic film based on Giono's short story.

A bakery also forms the centerpiece of Eric Rohmer's film *La*

Boulangère de Monceau (The Bakery Girl of Monceau). A budding romance takes place between the upper-class protagonist and a working-class woman who sells pastries at a bakery. Every day, he returns to the bakery to order one, two, or more *sablés* (sugar cookies), which become the erotic focus of the protagonist, the bakery clerk, and the viewers. The narrator calls a halt to the would-be romance when faced with more suitable prey, but the bakery also serves as a backdrop for the new paramour.

Finally, in the short story "La légende du pain" (The Legend of Bread), Michel Tournier recounts a fable: Two towns in Brittany get into an almost irreconcilable conflict when a native son and daughter plan their wedding. The bride and the groom both want their own village's bread for the festivities. This dilemma leads us to the development of a new kind of compromise bread for the wedding, becoming a creation myth for . . . *le pain au chocolat* (the chocolate croissant)!

If we are looking for further proof of the central role of bread in French daily life, we need only turn to language:

A job is known as a *gagne-pain* (earn bread).

Il y a du pain sur la planche (There's bread on the board) means there is work to be done.

Elle a mangé le pain du roi (She ate the king's bread) signifies "She went to prison."

Il a plus de la moitié de son pain cuit (More than half his bread is cooked) means "He doesn't have much longer to live."

Bread, in other words, equals life.

When a French village loses its bakery in the present day, the event borders on tragedy. The sole bakery in La Chapelle-en-Juger in Normandy closed its doors in 2017. On a sunny day in September 2019, eighty people held a demonstration in front of the defunct bakery, demanding its reopening. "The bakery is the social media of the community, a place of life. There is gossip, there are funny stories, it's going to rain, it's not going to rain. You don't need to go on the internet to find that out, you just go to the bakery," declared Nicolas Bourdier, a resident of La Chapelle-en-Juger. But for the past few years, the inhabitants of this village were obliged to drive ten kilometers to get their daily *baguette*, and life was not the same. Other villages have also resorted to demonstrations, flash mobs, dances, and songs to will their defunct bakeries back into existence. Believing that big business and supermarkets were forcing small bakers out of business, demonstrators hoped to capture the attention of the media so that someone would purchase the premises and fire up the ovens again. The strategy seems to have worked. Today La Chapelle-en-Juger boasts a bakery called Oh Saveurs d'Antan (Oh, the Tastes of Long Ago), and it seems to be thriving.

Some claim that the death knell for villages threatens to resound throughout the French countryside, but a new movement is being born: "permaculture," based on natural ecosystems. Even before the global pandemic, some young people were headed from congested cities to the open air to live a life more in tune with their values of respecting the earth, people, and the equitable distribution of resources. A new program called Erasmus Rural, named after the European Erasmus program that allows students to study in another country for a semester or a year, places students in the French countryside doing volunteer work for several months. And some of them get hooked, as permaculture's mantra claims: "Instead of waiting for the world to change, we could change the world."

L'Avenir est dans les œufs (*The Future Is in Eggs*), one of Eugène Ionesco's famous absurdist plays, was first produced in 1957 in Paris. The title at first seems farcical, but upon second thought, especially after the onset of the pandemic, it seems less absurd than ever. More people now believe that the future may well lie in farms, chickens, and eggs. If you saw the classic American film *The Graduate*, you'll remember the moment when the character Mr. McGuire whispers in Benjamin's ear the magic word "Plastics," the field of the future. Today, the equivalent may indeed be "Eggs."

Inhabitants of small towns in France also report increasing satisfaction with their quality of life. Take, for example, Château Gontier, a community of seventeen thousand about three hundred kilometers to the southwest of Paris, where, according to some of its inhabitants, the economy is thriving and residents are contented and engaged. *"Un havre de paix"* (a peaceful haven) is how the owner of a cement factory and a handball coach describes the place. It is *"un petit oasis,"* notes the director of the local theater—no unemployment, insecurity, or traffic jams . . . but the residents do have a hospital, a theater, a conservatory, a cinema, and many organizations working for social good. While it lacks the myriad options found in a big city at any given moment, how many choices does anyone really need?

URBAN NEIGHBORHOODS

French neighborhoods provide an excellent example of belonging and of joie de vivre in daily life. It's already something to be smug about if your postal code begins with 75—representing Paris proper, not the *banlieue* (suburbs), which are sometimes considered worlds unto themselves—but the 75 postal code is far from being homogenous.

Neighborhoods are everything in Paris—a series of villages, as some have described them. You will know the salespeople at your neighborhood bakery, the vendor running the little fruit and vegetable shops, and what some still call the *Arabe du coin* (the Arab on the corner)—most of the Parisian convenience stores seem to be owned by first- or second-generation North African immigrants. When the term was first coined, it seemed reductive and potentially derogatory, but now many such shopkeepers have reclaimed and reappropriated the moniker. In his novel *Black Bazaar*, the Franco-Congolese author Alain Mabanckou fittingly portrays the Parisian *Arabe du coin* as friend of the neighborhood, amateur psychologist, and dispenser of wisdom. My favorite *Arabe du coin* (as he jokingly calls himself), Rachid, runs a fruit market in the rue Campagne Première near Montparnasse. The street, named after a general in the first battle of the French Revolution, Alexandre Taponier, is known as the site not of military history but of the last scene of Jean-Luc Godard's emblematic New Wave film *Breathless*. The protagonist, played by Jean-Paul Belmondo, is shot in the back as he runs to escape from police, but he continues to stagger down the rue Campagne Première to the corner of the boulevard Raspail, where he succumbs while mumbling a few final, enigmatic words. Cinema buffs flock to this street to reconstruct this iconic scene in their imaginations.

But back to Rachid and his fruit market.

Rachid once told me of his blue-sky, family-filled vacations in his native Tunisia, where he loved to visit but not to stay, as he was now established in France. He patiently explained to me the differences among tangerines, mandarins, and clementines, and among Bosc, D'Anjou, and Comice pears. From time to time, he would make homemade soups with just the right amount of *ras el hanout* (a North African spice mix that includes cardamom, turmeric, cumin, ginger, and chili peppers) to sell during the winter. Near the cash register he kept raw almonds, almond paste, and candied ginger, meant to tempt weak-willed souls. When I told him that his cunning strategy always worked on me, he held his head back and laughed heartily.

One day, as I was poring yet again over a panoply of pears, a wealthily dressed woman came into his little shop, grabbed a few fruits, slammed them on the counter, and asked for the price. Rachid kindly but firmly told her to wait, that he was busy helping another customer (even though I hadn't quite finished picking out my fruit). When he had methodically rung up my purchases and packed them away, he turned slowly to the now-impatient woman and said in his gentlest voice, "Now, may I help you, madame?" Like the "Arab on the corner" in Mabanckou's novel, Rachid, the nicest *Arabe du coin*, as he calls himself, remains loyal to his neighborhood crew.

In your own neighborhood, you have *your* métro stops, *your* shops, and *your* park—from the Square René Le Gall in the 13th arrondissement to the Palais Royal in the 2nd to the Parc Monceau in the 17th. Sometimes you even recognize and greet the same checkers at your nearest Monoprix or Carrefour (supermarkets), although, like everywhere in the industrialized world, these jobs are being progressively replaced by computerized self-checkout stations. Most French people, though they may shop in supermarkets for such items as laundry soap and canned or frozen goods, continue to support small local merchants—cheese and butcher shops, fish markets, wine sellers, bakeries, fruit and vegetable markets. Even *tabacs*, those ancient tobacco shops that still sell cigarettes, chewing tobacco, and lottery tickets, continue to flourish and, now, keeping up with the times, offer prepaid mobile phone subscriptions, too. Each time I go to France, I reconnect with those shopkeepers in my old neighborhood or make the acquaintance of those around me wherever I may be staying, a practice that adds moments of pleasure to each encounter.

THE UNDERDOG

When you think of heroes who define Frenchness, who comes to mind? Perhaps the three musketeers or the Count of Monte Cristo. Maybe Charles de Gaulle, whom the French voted as their hero just a few years ago on the television show *The Greatest French Person of All Time*. Perhaps Marie Curie, a fearless, pioneering scientist and the first woman to win the Nobel Prize. (Actually, she won two of them.) But I would like to suggest a different model, someone who more subtly and more broadly represents Frenchness: the underdog.

When Edmond Rostand's play *Cyrano de Bergerac* premiered in Paris in 1897, France had just been defeated in the Franco-Prussian War and had suffered further through the anti-Semitic, morale-sapping Dreyfus Affair. In the midst of this national crisis, Rostand feared on opening night that his play would be a complete flop. But when the curtain descended at the end of the play and then rose again, there erupted the longest standing ovation in French history. Reports of its duration vary from twenty minutes to an hour, but the audience response was unequivocally *du jamais vu* (unprecedented). One spectator, the minister of finance, was so moved that he ripped off his own

Legion of Honor insignia and pinned it on Rostand's lapel. He needn't have bothered: Rostand was himself presented with that highest French order of merit at the play's next performance.

Granted, the play's lead character, formulated in late-nineteenth-century Paris, may not be entirely reproduceable in the twenty-first century. But why was the audience so taken with him? And how does Cyrano define Frenchness, even today?

Cyrano de Bergerac is at once courageous and timid, strong and vulnerable, conniving and sincere, uncompromising and sensitive, a bumbling stammerer and a brilliant slam poet, a lover and a friend. In short, he is a living paradox—not unlike many of us. However, his long nose makes him unattractive (I empathize), so he has no hope of winning over Roxane. Instead, he agrees to write eloquent love letters in the voice of the handsome but rather doltish Christian, whom Roxane chooses as her beau. After many adventures, Cyrano's true identity as the author of the brilliant letters is revealed, and Roxane declares her love for the dying Cyrano.

Should we draw the conclusion from the play's ending that wit, integrity, loyalty, eloquence, and panache will eventually triumph over beauty? Some believe so. But the question is undoubtedly more complicated. How can we know whether Roxane would have fallen for Cyrano earlier, when he was not dying, had she known he was the true author of the letters?

Love and attraction are strange things, but Cyrano de Bergerac remains a profoundly human hero in the annals of French history and in the present. The play, with all its spin-off films, comics, podcasts, and video games, continues to enchant audiences with its virtuoso language, its sense of adventure, and its humanity.

Part of Cyrano's appeal today lies in his androgyny. He is stereotypically masculine in his swashbuckling swordsmanship and military prowess and stereotypically feminine in his devotion and undemanding love. (Cue Penelope awaiting Ulysses.) His virtuosity as a poet and his probity are not gendered, and he remains continually self-questioning and vulnerable. These qualities are undoubtedly part of his charm, as is his lack of overwrought masculinity in his relationship with Roxane. As a counterweight to his force stands his weakness.

The importance of acknowledging and even embracing weakness has gained quite a bit of traction by the French public in recent years, as evidenced by sales of Swiss author Alexandre Jollien's book *L'Éloge de la faiblesse* (In Praise of Weakness). What does it mean to be "disabled"? And even more pertinent, what if we are all disabled in some way? Born with cerebral palsy, Jollien explores in his work the meaning of disability, weakness, and suffering. Through philosophy and meditation, he studies how to improve one's condition and, barring that, how to accept it. This philosophical self-help allows one to find joy even when obstacles arise. In another book, *La Sagesse espiègle* (Mischievous Wisdom), Jollien examines the idea that life will inevitably be messy, but that's as it should be.

In reading Jollien's dictum *"C'est le bordel, mais il n'y a pas de problème"* (It's a mess, but there's no problem), I was reminded of a trip I took to Mopti, Mali, with students a few years ago. The name of the hole-in-the-wall hotel where we stayed was Y'a Pas de Problème (There's No Problem). Seriously. You can only imagine the bad jokes the students, my friend Chérif, and I concocted:

"There are no sheets? *Pas de problème!"*

"The wall has just caved in? *Pas de problème!"* and so on.

But back to Jollien's version of "no problem," which was inspired by Nietzsche. In order for humans to understand health, they must first experience sickness. But Jollien, again following

Nietzsche, argues that the conditions of health and sickness are not opposites, as innumerable forms of health exist that incorporate disability and a wide variety of conditions. Only through this understanding, he argues, can we arrive at a state of true health.

The oh-so-French Serge Gainsbourg wrote a classic song, "Des laids des laids" (The Ugly Ones) that echoes both Cyrano and Jollien:

> *Enfin faut faire avec c'qu'on a*
> *Notre sale gueule mais on n'y peut rien*
> *D'ailleurs nous les affreux*
> *J'suis sûr que Dieu nous accorde*
> *Un peu de sa miséricorde car*
> *La beauté cachée des laids, des laids*
> *Se voit sans délai, délai.*
> *(In the end, we must make do with what we have / An ugly*
> *face, but we can't do anything about it. / But I'm sure that*
> *God grants / Mercy to us ugly ones, because / Our hidden*
> *beauty can immediately be seen.)*

The pages of French literary history are filled with underdogs who triumph in some way: La Fontaine, inspired by Aesop and others, describes in his fables the Tortoise beating the Hare to the finish line, the Oyster eating the Rat, and the meager Reed outlasting the mighty Oak. Dorine, the servant in Molière's *Tartuffe*, outthinks all the higher-class characters, and Victor Hugo's Quasimodo captures the hearts of readers and viewers on an international scale. Contemporary Francophone writers from Marie NDiaye to Roukiata Ouedraogo recount stories of immigrant women who face seemingly insurmountable challenges. Like

La Fontaine's flexible reed, they overcome adversity by their dexterity.

By embracing weakness as a foundation of humanity, along with potential and strength, these figures—along with Cyrano, the intellectual, the sensitive swordsman—personify an important form of Frenchness.

THE POWER OF DEBATE

After living in France for a few years, I was forcibly faced with a reverse cultural misunderstanding. My American friend Amelia had come to Paris for a visit, and she, my French friend Jacques, and I all went out for a coffee on the rue Mouffetard just south of the Latin Quarter.

At the time, Jacques was a film location manager who, among other things, had found and arranged to transport one hundred sheep to appear in a television ad for laundry detergent. Amelia spoke no French, so our conversation took place in English. As we sipped our espressos at an outdoor table perched on cobblestones, we entered into deep reflections on various countries' religious traditions, growing animated and engaged, our challenges and repartees flying about.

Amelia suddenly brought the conversation to a halt by blurting out, "You aren't really interested in what I think, are you?"

Jacques and I were both dumbstruck.

"What? Where did that come from?"

Backing up a bit, I realized what had just happened—it was a problem of communication based on cultural expectations. In French conversation, you counter opinions with other opinions, evidence with other evidence, and there's no sense that your personhood is in any way threatened just because your inter-locutor doesn't agree with you. On the contrary, French children are taught to defend themselves from an early age, even against their parents: "You liked that movie? Why? I didn't think it was very interesting . . ."

My mistake with Amelia was in not showing more American-style sensitivity. I had fallen into the local French mode of dis-cussion, in which you are allowed, *expected*, to advance an idea or an argument forcefully for its own sake without its being mis-taken for a personal attack. It's completely liberating—water off a *canard*'s back. I had blithely been operating from another set of cultural rules, but that fact in no way justified hurting the feelings of a friend. I sincerely apologized. However, this mis-understanding didn't stop me from thinking that the French approach to discussion has definite advantages.

In both private and public life, the French generally do not deny controversial questions by sweeping them under the rug. Instead, the issues are exposed and brought forward for debate. As an example, early depictions of the Second World War attempted to shunt all the blame onto the Germans, but the importance of French involvement in wartime atrocities is now repeatedly recognized. Historical plaques on all French public schools from which Jewish children were deported now explicitly state that the children were taken with the consent of the (French) Vichy government. And the 2001 "Loi Taubira" (a law named after the French-Guianan minister of justice who proposed it) declared the slave trade and slavery to be crimes against humanity, both of which are now included in France's not-often-discussed history.

More recently, President Emmanuel Macron publicly apolo-gized for the torture of separatist Algerians during the Algerian

War of Independence (1957–62), which previous governments had vociferously denied. By the time Algeria gained independence from French colonial rule in 1962, roughly 400,000 Algerian and 35,000 French lives had been lost. In 2022 Macron, in collaboration with Algerian president Abelmadjid Tebboune, established a commission composed of French and Algerian historians to investigate "the reconciliation between French and Algerian people." The commission will make use of a recent report on Franco-Algerian relations by Benjamin Stora, one of France's most eminent historians. Born in Algeria to Jewish parents, Stora immigrated to France at the age of twelve, participated in the social upheavals of May 1968, and ultimately became a professor at the Université Sorbonne Paris Nord. His work focuses on collective memory and the history of Algeria. Some say he has spent his life remembering a war that France has tried to forget.

France's reckoning with its colonial past has been slow in coming: only at the turn of the twenty-first century was the War of Algerian Independence included in school textbooks. Stora argues that the traumatization of French society because of that war is like a sordid "family secret," and that denial eats away at the body politic like a cancer. The joint commission seeks to uncover truths about the war and false claims originating from both sides. Despite criticisms of the project, it is hoped that the commission will conduct a lucid inquiry into France's collective amnesia, thereby reconciling the "memorial conflicts" that continue today, even among young people born long after the war ended.

France is not alone in its recognition of past misdeeds, but its established culture of debate seems to invite this sort of reckoning. In December 2020, the French legislature voted for an act of possible restitution, which granted a return of the Sword of Omar Tall to Senegal and King Béhanzin's treasures to Benin. These acts mark the beginning of responding to the many requests to return African artwork acquired—many would argue "pillaged"—during the colonial period (1830–1962). The French minister of culture has insisted that this law in no way allows all art to be returned upon demand; it simply permits a commission to study each request. Previous law had declared the "inalienability principle of the patrimony code"—meaning: *Don't mess with stuff that belongs to France*. But thanks to the very French tradition of argument and debate, the domain of cultural heritage is at last being shaken up, especially regarding artifacts confiscated during the colonial period.

Even though controversy has always been a part of public life in the land of Voltaire, I've often wondered why the French hold so many labor strikes. There are of course historical explanations, but the incorporation of controversy in the public sphere (much like raising children to be able to argue) brings about an explicit, ongoing airing of differences. And sometimes the strikes produce important results.

The SNCF (railroad) strike in 2019/20 against proposed changes to retirement law resulted in the withdrawal of the government's proposal. While the "Yellow Vests" (*Gilets jaunes*) do not represent a specific labor movement, their 2018 protests succeeded in forcing the government to drop its proposed gas tax, whose burden would have fallen unduly on the working class living outside Paris's city limits. The movement subsequently made amorphous demands, some more reasonable than others, and lost momentum, but the fact remains that its first protests saw measurable results.

Back to those French children who are taught to face resistance from the outset: They become adults who don't shy away from conflict. As a result, bumps in the road seem more manageable. And maybe most important, engaging in debate and arguments—even Daedalian ones—makes for more nimble thinkers. And the process can be both effective and exhilarating.

PUBLIC SCHOOLS

Our daughters, Lise and Laura, grew up "partially French" by attending public schools in Paris for three years. When I directed programs abroad, they came, too, and even though my husband couldn't be with us during the entire time, he embraced the idea as a priceless experience for them. Both of us would have relished the opportunity to grow up bilingual ourselves.

Any public school system in the world reveals reams about the wider culture's values, and French schools are no exception. Whereas my colleagues had chosen to place their children in private bilingual schools while they were in Paris (with which they were all reasonably satisfied), it seemed to us that the real way to experience French education (and to become truly bilingual) would be in a French public school, even though the learning curve would be steep—and sometimes painful.

Our daughters' first school, the École élémentaire Buffon (Buffon Elementary School), near the Jardin des Plantes, was immortalized in Robert Doisneau's photos of the 1940s. Over fifty years later, the two-child desks had been updated, but the rest remained almost exactly as it was in Doisneau's day.

It was in these memorialized rooms that Lise and Laura, with three years separating them, began the *maternelle* (kindergarten).

When Lise, our elder daughter, first walked into the *maternelle* classroom, her first thought was clear: *Wow, do I have a lot of work to do to catch up with all these kids speaking French!* Three years later, Laura, our younger daughter, however, took a different tack: *Wow, do I have a lot of work to do to teach all these kids English!* We had spoken some French at home, and we often had French or Francophone African houseguests, so she understood virtually everything being said. It was just that school wasn't supposed to be in French. Still, Laura made every effort to pantomime or gesture while resolutely speaking English.

The other children were at first baffled by her. One little boy with tousled dark hair and missing front teeth, Thibault, came over to us on the first day and said helpfully, *"Je parle anglais."*

To which I responded: *"Ah, bon?"* (Really?)

"Oui," he replied. *"Sheet."* He smiled. *"Sheet* is a bad word," he continued in French, snickering, "but it's the only English word I know."

"Tu veux dire un drap?" (Do you mean a sheet?), I teasingly inquired.

"No. *Sheet,"* Thibault insisted, chortling.

I gently suggested that he might want to work on the short-*i* sound in English (as in "big" and "pig"), if he wanted to impress his future Anglophone friends with swear words.

It wasn't long before Laura was included in the courtyard games of *chat* (hide-and-seek) and begrudgingly began to communicate with the children in their own language. When she returned to French schools in CM1 (fourth grade), her new teacher would be Monsieur Coty (a weathered Breton sailor who looked as though he had stepped out of a nineteenth-century photograph).

"Oui, madame," he warned me. "I will accept Laura in my

class, but I can tell you right now that there is not a chance that she will be promoted to the next grade at the end of the year."

"That's no problem," I replied in French. "It will be a learning experience for her, and that's all we're asking."

The year began with great difficulty, particularly given that Laura's elementary school in the United States minimized the importance of grades, whereas in France, not only did every point count, but the students were also ranked in order of their achievement: "First in the class, second in the class," and so on. This practice, glorious for some and excruciating for others, has thankfully disappeared for the most part, but it was in full force at the time. A French friend of mine who teaches third grade in a Parisian school told me that while the ranking is no longer announced in class, students can still consult an online version of class averages with student ID numbers to learn exactly where they stand in relation to everyone else. The practice of ranking continues, but it has become less blatant.

Laura was not first, but "last in the class"—at least at the beginning. Her first *dictée* (a common practice in which the teacher reads a passage, and the students transcribe it word for word) was not quite a complete disaster: 2 points out of 10. But even if she understood the text, how would she write it? So many French words have unpronounced letters, like *vieux* (meaning "old," with its silent *x*); or the name of her new friend, Thibault of "sheet" fame (with a silent *h*, *l*, and final *t*); or *eau* ("water," pronounced "oh," a word that appears to have nothing to do with the sounds made by *e* or *a* or *u*). In short, *dictées* were delivered by the devil, even for French pupils, so what was a foreigner to do?

Fortunately, *dictées* were not the only things that were graded. Physical education, art, singing, and poetry recitation were also evaluated on a score of 1 to 10. Laura loved both song and poetry, so she enthusiastically prepared for those recitations and sometimes ended up with a 9.5 or a 10/10, which counterbalanced the lamentable *dictée* grade. She also loved history, which forms a considerable part of the early French public school curriculum, beginning with the Gauls in 500 BCE. By fourth grade, pupils have made it to the French Renaissance, the period into which Laura landed one year. For her upcoming test, Lise and I shot questions at Laura for practice. She finally learned the name of the horrific mass murder of Protestants during the Wars of Religion of 1562–98, Le Massacre de la Saint-Barthélemy (the Saint Bartholomew's Day Massacre), and she practiced the pronunciation many times until she got it right. Then back to the questioning:

"Who was the king of France in the sixteenth century?"

"Saint Barthélemy?" she queried.

"Who wrote the famous book *Gargantua*?" I asked, referring to Rabelais's work.

"Saint-Barthélemy!"

Years later, when we have no clue as to the answer for a question, someone in our family will inevitably chime in "Saint Barthélemy?" The saint's day of that grim historical event has been repurposed into a lasting family memento.

If you were lucky enough to have an enterprising and fearless teacher at the École Buffon, you had the opportunity to go on a *classe de neige* (a ski trip) or a *classe de mer* (trip to the sea). As befits a Breton sailor, Monsieur Coty volunteered to take Laura's class to the Île d'Yeu, off the Brittany coast, to study sea life and learn the rudiments of sailing. His request for funding from the Ministry of Education was approved, much to the joy of the children.

At age nine, Laura had never been away from home except

for brief sleepovers, and she would be gone for ten days, which seemed like an eternity to me. As she boarded the bus, I could feel my heart drop with a never-before-experienced melancholy. But I appeared to be the only one concerned—Laura was by then happily chattering in French with her *camarades*. With parents enthusiastically waving goodbye, the bus headed from the rue Buffon to the seashore some seven hours away.

The days flew by as the children observed the movement of crabs on the beach and learned how to direct the sails of a catamaran. They exulted in the ocean, the easily available bicycles to tour the island, and the fresh sea breezes. Some of them had never seen the ocean before. In the cabin, Laura shared a room with her two best friends, Marianne and Kelli, who together painted a rather typical picture of the Parisian population of today. Marianne is the daughter of a Frenchwoman and a Lebanese man, and Kelli was born in France to parents from the Central African Republic, a former French colony.

Although there continued to be challenges for the *petite Américaine* that year, Laura counts the École Buffon as one of her key life experiences. At the end of the year, Monsieur Coty called me aside at the *kermesse* (the end-of-school carnival). "Madame," he avowed, "I was wrong. Laura will easily be promoted to the next grade." Granted, she had worked at it, but she had also become a product of the French school system, in which children are prodded by attentive teachers to make progress in the company of peers who are "all in it together."

When Laura's older sister, Lise, returned to École Buffon in third grade (CE2), she was placed next to Nahil, who was *première de la classe* (first in the class). The teacher assumed that an excellent student who wasn't struggling herself would be able to help *la petite Américaine* (somehow, this label kept appearing).

Nahil was the perfect child, with perfectly coiffed long brown braids, a crisp plaid skirt, and a white blouse. Maybe even the teacher's pet. But it turned out she was also universally appreciated, selected by her classmates to be the *déléguée de classe* (class representative). For the longest time after Lise's arrival, the teacher allowed the two of them to whisper to each other softly, in case Lise missed any instructions or important points. It took the teacher two months to realize that, after a while, the girls were simply chatting, but when she did, their desk partnership was brought to an abrupt halt, and Lise and Nahil were paired with other students, much to their disappointment. But the *complicité* had already been established, and despite the now-distant desks, the friendship continued to blossom.

Fast-forwarding to high school, Lise was able to attend the Lycée Montaigne (Montaigne High School) thanks to Nahil's mother, Françoise (aka Gwenda), who had kindly made the arrangements. Situated just across from the Jardin du Luxembourg in Paris, the Lycée Montaigne counts among its illustrious alumni Roland Barthes and Jean-Paul Sartre. Every morning, when Lise got past the guards and arrived at the school's courtyard, she'd marvel at the very French ritual that played out as each student entered the grounds. Two girls would greet each other with a *bise* (a kiss on each cheek). Then a third would arrive, kiss the other two, and assume her place, forming a triangle . . . which soon became a square with the arrival of a fourth . . . who would kiss the other three. Then a fifth would arrive, kissing the other four, one by one, and transforming the geometric shape into a circle. This n+1 ritual would continue, each new arrival kissing every other girl who had arrived before her, with sometimes as many as twelve or fourteen girls all repeating the ritual and now forming something resembling a lopsided parallelepiped. Lise noted that this was a friendly way to start the day, even though any given conversation could never last more than a few seconds before it was interrupted and restructured.

As a teenager, Nahil spent several summers with us in Minnesota, hiking, singing, camping out, eating roasted marshmallows (*chamallows*), going to amusement parks, and checking out the boys downtown with Lise. Each time we returned to France, Nahil would greet Lise as her wayfaring best friend, and the two would become inseparable once again.

The French often think of Americans as friendly and outgoing when you first meet them but see that friendliness as only skin-deep. My friend Marie from the *banlieue* of Paris theorizes that French people are coconuts, and Americans are peaches. Americans are soft on the outside and hard on the inside, and the French are the other way around. If an American spends an evening talking with someone at a party, that doesn't mean that the two are going to become good friends or that the American will invite that person into her home, or even contact her again. Rarely do we include our friends in every aspect of our lives.

But in France, the belief is that as soon as you begin to have repeated conversations, you are becoming friends. And when you become friends, it's assumed to be a long-term prospect. Some of my current friends in France date from my first year as a student there; others, from the period when our children were quite young. If you can generalize on the subject, the French tend to be extremely loyal friends. Years after Lise and Nahil sat together at their wooden desks at the École Buffon, Nahil flew across the Atlantic to be the maid of honor in Lise's wedding. Their younger sisters, Marianne and Laura, also became fast friends and are continuing their friendship into the future.

Teachers in the French public school system were once stereotypically severe, accepting no flak from students. Even art is a
serious matter to be studied and perfected. In elementary school
art classes in the United Staes, Lise's teachers were consistently
encouraging, along the lines of "That's a nice horse. . . . Oh,
it's not a horse? Well, okay, but it has lovely colors." In France,
though, art classes were a horse of a different color. "That's supposed to be a unicorn? It doesn't look like a unicorn—the horn
is coming out of the chin, the legs are longer than the body,
and unicorns aren't turquoise and pink. Go back and work on
it some more." The result was that Lise, both of whose parents
can scarcely draw a stick figure, once ended up producing a
stunning winged Pegasus that continued to hang in her room
well after all the other childhood artwork had been expunged.

When I asked Lise and Laura the major differences they
saw between French and American public education, after they
had experienced both systems, they had a variety of responses.
While both countries include group work meant to encourage
collaboration among students, Laura noted that, in France, the
teacher's job is to present the material, and it is the student's
responsibility to be engaged and to learn. In the United States,
she said, the teacher's job is to make the subjects interesting
and even entertaining. Lise adds that while the French system
is more highly structured, in the American system, "anything
goes" much more often than in French schools, for better or for
worse. The result is that the American classroom can be more
relaxed, but the French approach teaches more independence
and accountability. One could argue that, in the French system, the joy of learning must ultimately come from within.
The added emphasis on personal responsibility might account
for the fact that French youth are considered adults at eighteen

and have almost all privileges accorded to twenty-one-year-olds in the United States.

Ultimately, though, Lise and Laura agree that an ideal educational system would combine elements from both countries: high standards with limited pressure; seriousness of purpose with enjoyment (and Laura would decidedly recommend keeping the three recesses that French children enjoy!).

IN DEFENSE OF THE FRENCH LANGUAGE

Oui, j'ai une patrie. La langue française.
(Yes, I have a homeland. The French language.)
—Albert Camus

La langue française est une femme. Et cette femme est si belle, si fière, si modeste, si hardie, touchante, voluptueuse, chaste, noble, familière, folle, sage, qu'on l'aime de toute son âme, et qu'on n'est jamais tenté de lui être infidèle.
(The French language is a woman. And this woman is so beautiful, so proud, so modest, so daring, touching, voluptuous, chaste, noble, familiar, crazy, wise, that you love her with all your soul, and you are never tempted to be unfaithful to her.)
—Anatole France

Despite the diversity of ideas and cultures now coexisting in France, it would be difficult to convince most French people that their language is not the linguistic center of the universe. Have any citizens in the history of humanity been prouder or more chauvinistic about their own language than the French?

Until about the sixteenth century, Latin was the only "serious" language in France—legal, religious, and scientific works were published in that ancient tongue. But during the sixteenth century, French began to gain ground as the principal written language. The Edict of Villers-Cotterêts of 1539 established it as the official language of the kingdom. Different forms of French (as well as Breton, Basque, Alsatian, and other regional languages) were still spoken, but the written language, *le françois*, was on its way to becoming standardized. "Bastard" eventually became *bâtard*, "cognoisseur" became *connaisseur*, and *amour*, unchanged, was recognized throughout the land.

The real force of the Edict of Villers-Cotterêts lay in its nationalist designs—French would now be held in the same esteem as Latin. Articles 110 and 111 of the treaty constitute the oldest legislation still applicable in France today: 110 specifies that governmental decrees must be clear and understandable (good luck with that one!), and 111 requires that all legal documents must be drawn up in the French language. In a parallel move toward decipherability, some of the first French translations of the Bible were printed in the 1530s. However, because the Catholic king François I forbade vernacular translations of the sacred texts, they were printed in Belgium and Switzerland but widely circulated in France.

Another French nationalist movement was taking shape in the literary world of the Renaissance: in 1549, the diplomat and poet Joachim du Bellay published *La Deffence et illustration de la langue françoise* (Defense and Illustration of the French Language). At that time, *illustration* meant "to make illustrious," and du Bellay urged French poets to write in French (not in neo-Latin) and to hold their own against (and even surpass) the Latin, Greek, and Italian poets. Du Bellay's call to arms did not go unheeded: some of the most exquisite lyrical French verse of all time was written by a circle of poets called La Pléiade (named after the constellation the Pleiades), headed by Pierre de Ronsard and seconded by du Bellay himself. La Pléiade made the French language proud.

Today, French remains an important international language, with roughly three hundred million speakers worldwide. After English, French is the second most taught language, and French and English are the only two languages spoken on five major continents. L'Académie française (the French Academy) was founded during the reign of Louis XIII in 1635 to preserve, perfect, and standardize the French language. Although its quasi-divine status among the French populace has faded in recent years, it still decides such life-or-death matters as whether you should pronounce the *s* in *les* before *haricots*, as in *les haricots verts* (green beans). For the record, now you can pronounce the phrase "lez haricots," whereas, if you had said that ten years ago, you would have been fit to be sent to the cultural guillotine.

For some linguistic purists, the Académie has relinquished control to the unruly populace by accepting as standard French such terms as *antiraciste*, from English; *machiste* (macho), from Spanish; and *barbouze* (a military counterinsurgent in the Algerian War of Independence), from Arabic. Still, even though it is completely out of step with natural linguistic evolution, the Académie française forges on, valiantly defending the purity of the French language—forty musketeers fending off an army of millions.

If you have learned another language, you have probably had the experience of saying something quite different from what you *thought* you were saying. When I was learning French in high school, I was glad to learn that after the *t* in *est* (is), you make the link with the following word if it begins with a vowel. So, *elle est ici* (she is here) is pronounced "el eh teecee." So, when we were going to view the classic 1966 film *Un homme et une femme* (*A Man and a Woman*), by Claude Lelouch, I announced with great pride, to the amusement of French speakers around me, that I looked forward to seeing "Un homme *est* une femme," essentially saying, "A Man *Is* a Woman"—and this took place well before the word *transgender* became common currency. But that was far from my worst blunder. Once, when asked at dinner if I would like a second serving, I responded, *"Non, merci. Je suis pleine"* (literally: "I am full"). However, it turns out that, in French, the expression means "I am a pregnant animal." Imagine, then, the surprise of the French host families when an American male student inevitably says, "Je suis plein"! This anglicism, however, has begun to be more acceptable in recent years.

A more dangerous mistake that both I and my women students have made at some point is "Je suis chaude" (literally: "I am hot"). Unfortunately, the expression has erotic implications, particularly when spoken by a woman, and means something like "I'm raring to go and ready for sex."

But probably my most egregious mistake occurred during a conversation about food additives. I sincerely inquired whether the jam on the table had any *préservatifs* in it. You can only imagine the hilarity of all the listeners—what I had asked meant "Does this jam have any *condoms* in it?" No, they assured me, it did not.

One good way to improve your French is to read Tolstoy's novels in English translation. The trick is that they aren't entirely in English, as upper-class Russians of the nineteenth century were so enamored of all things French that their novels are riddled with untranslated French expressions and sentences. I learned from Tolstoy's *Anna Karenina* that *primesautier* means "spontaneous" or "impulsive." I don't recall for certain, but it probably describes the rogue character Vronsky, who suspiciously resembles Flaubert's Rodolphe in *Madame Bovary*, written some twenty years earlier. But, seriously, if you pick up a copy of *War and Peace* in an English translation that faithfully follows the original, you will encounter, as you flip through the pages, quite a lot of French—that's part of what kept me plowing through the hefty volume one summer.

I've always been fascinated with the borrowing of expressions from different languages, but more important, why we do so. What do those expressions evoke that English words don't suffice to describe? From Spanish, we borrow *burrito*, and from Italian, *gelato*, and from French, *croissant*. No contest, right? They all describe something unique to those cultures. But what about the expression *je ne sais quoi*? Are the French inscrutable? Do they have a certain something that no one else can describe?

And then there are words borrowed from another language that simply don't mean what they're supposed to mean in English. *Double-entendre*, with the clever, "wink, wink" quality we assign to it, does not exist as such in French; it simply signifies a double meaning. The expression *à double sens* is much more common. *À la mode*, for the French, simply means "in style" or "trendy," so "pie à la mode" technically has nothing to do with ice cream. (Although, I guess you could argue that ice cream is always fashionable.) If you were to yell *"Encore!"* (Again!) at the end of a French concert, the performers might imagine that you wanted them simply to repeat the last song. *"Une autre!"* (Another!) is the French expression you want—which, when you think about it, makes a lot more sense.

After having lived in France for about three years at the time, when you add up my various stays, my aspiration to become French had faded somewhat. Picture this: I am at a birthday party for my daughter Lise's friend—ten candles—and I am chatting with various parents about recent decisions by the FCPE (Fédération des conseils de parents d'élèves). Others contended that we should instead attend the meetings of PEEP (Parents d'élèves de l'enseignement public), a body more aligned with social change. I had imagined that these organizations might resemble a local American Parent Teacher Association, with an exchange of ideas, but when I eventually attended meetings for both, it turned out that they were much more like union meetings, with a list of demands to be presented to the school administration.

After a while, one of the fathers at the birthday party came over to me and said quietly in French, "You have a secret. I'm not sure what it is, but you have a secret."

Curious, I asked, also in French, "What sort of secret?"

"You have roots from elsewhere in your background, but I can't figure out where. You're keeping the secret well, though."

"It's no secret. I'm American."

"American? You mean, *really* American?"

"That's right. No secret."

"I assumed you didn't want anyone to know what other roots you might have. But I picked up something strange when you used the word *dramatique*, which is generally used only in a theatrical context and not to describe a sunset in French."

Busted! Ah, the tribulations of not being French . . .

Desperately trying to be French will inevitably fail, but if you manage to "pass" on occasion while not paying attention, you can still get it wrong. I love this country, but the asymptotic curve toward Frenchness is infinite—you get closer and closer, but you never arrive.

I learned almost all the French swear words I know in the passenger seat of a car. One day, a group of us were riding in a car with my French host brother Bruno on a mountainous road near Valence, in southern France. As we advanced in the narrow lane, another car was riding our back bumper and eventually succeeded in passing us. Furious because of the danger involved, Bruno decided to pass the driver himself to get even. (Don't even ask.) After this game of taking turns for a few rounds, windows were rolled down and new vocabulary words shot from car to car, echoing across the canyon:

"*Espèce de salaud!*" (Bastard!)

"*Con!*" (Literally, a vulgar term for female genitals, but in this context, "moron") . . .

While the rest of us were trying to talk Bruno down, the other car, now in front of us, stopped and blocked the road, forcing us to pull over. Both drivers flung open their doors and bounded outside. The other driver, wearing a rumpled brown shirt to match his rumpled brown hair, became a cheetah baring its teeth as he approached our car. Bruno, displaying his refusal to back down, advanced three steps. The cheetah and Bruno continued their less-than-amicable exchange, both gesticulating and turning brighter shades of crimson as they shouted even more new vocabulary words:

"*Enculé!*" ("Asshole," but it goes a bit farther than that.)

"*Enfoiré!*" ("Imbecile," from the word *foire*, for "diarrhea.")

Then, without explanation, Bruno concluded the discussion by throwing his hands up and pronouncing, "*Bon. C'est comme ça.*" (Okay, so that's the way it is.) Both men then spun around and returned to their respective driver's seats, as those of us in the car remained hauntingly silent to avoid escalating the duel. Each of the *combattants* proceeded to restart his car and calmly drive away, seemingly satisfied, as the rest of us exhaled a sigh of relief. It's not every day that you first fear for your life on a steep mountain road and then have the pleasure of learning thirty-some swear words in the space of five minutes.

Just when you think you know a lot of French, though, it turns out you don't.

When living in an apartment in Paris on my own during graduate school, although I could carry on a long conversation about, say, Proust, I discovered the hard way that I didn't know how to say the most basic things, like "lightbulb" (*ampoule*) or "socket" (*prise*). More recently, when one of the keys on my computer was malfunctioning, I realized that I didn't know the French word for that particular symbol. After a little research (and double-checking, as not all online resources are reliable), I headed to a computer store armed with my newly acquired French term: *barre oblique*. Easy enough, right? Making my way past the aisles laden with the latest in notebooks and laptops and USB drives, I at last arrived at the repair counter.

My problem, I explained to the technician, was with the *barre oblique*.

He looked at me blankly, as though I had just said "'Twas brillig, and the slithy toves . . ."

I repeated the term, trying to perfect my enunciation: "*Oui, la barre oblique.*"

After a few moments of furrowed brow and grimaces, his face lit up, "Ah, madame, you mean to say *le slash*!"

Yes, that's it. I meant to say *le slash*.

The French remain devoted to their language, and they love it when we foreigners occasionally get it just right.

6

Taking Time, Making Time

"Remember that time is money," Benjamin Franklin famously wrote in 1748, expressing a sentiment that would become one of the foundations of American life. "Managing" time, becoming more effective, and maximizing profit remain the catchphrases of today's work world in the United States. The French, however, have a different approach. The verb *profiter* is revealing—it looks like "to profit," but it actually means "to make the most of" or "to enjoy." This contrast speaks volumes about the two countries' differing attitudes toward time—as something to profit from or to enjoy. This distinction may at first glance seem dualistic, but I have found that, in its approach to history and to the world of work, French culture does bear it out.

In the land of Astérix, the Gallic warrior of comic strip fame, the sense of time is linked to history, and history permeates the present in France. The street names in Paris send the most casual walker to other eras: Vincent Auriol (president of France in the mid-twentieth century), Claude Debussy (a symbolist composer), Dora Bruder (a Jewish Parisian girl deported and killed in a

concentration camp in Germany during World War II), Marguerite de Navarre (a celebrated Renaissance writer), Sarah Bernhardt
(the preeminent nineteenth-century French actress), Jean-Baptiste
Lamarck (a pioneering eighteenth-century evolutionist), Léopold
Senghor (poet and first president of Senegal after its independence
from France). "How do you find your way around," my students
sometimes wonder, "when no streets are numbered?" (No Fifth
Street, no Seventh Avenue . . .) Well, for starters, Google Maps
notwithstanding, you learn at least some of the street names.

What does it mean to see monuments or the names of important historical figures on every corner every day? Somehow
it must impact your sense of the world when you pass by Notre
Dame, an 850-year-old edifice, on your way to work or to the
market. Even in the smallest French towns, there are ancient
cathedrals, monuments, and streets named after their most ven-
erable citizens.

How do the French imagine themselves following in the
footsteps of these cultural heroes and heroines? One possible
answer is that the icons from the past become a part of one's
present-day French identity. When Notre Dame was burning in
April 2019, I saw senior citizens and children alike weeping at
the sight—it is an inextricable part of their history and of their
place in the world.

A new French website, Paristique, a delight for devotees of etymology and history, allows you to click on many streets, parks,
and bridges in Paris to see the origins of their names. Some of
the entries contain less-than-earth-shattering revelations—as in
the Place des Fêtes, where, um, the people of Belleville used to
have parties; or the Pont au Change, near Notre Dame, where
visitors exchanged currency in medieval times. Other name origins are more fascinating: Who knew that boulevard Voltaire

was once named "Prince Eugène" after the Prince of Savoy and field marshal of the Holy Roman Empire and of the Hapsburg dynasty? But whereas the prince claimed naming rights for that important boulevard for only 13 years, the French philosopher of the Enlightenment has held the title for over 120 years (and still going strong)! There's an easy explanation for Voltaire's continuing claim on the street name: The pen is mightier than the sword.

History and time are woven together in other ways. The "French paradox" has been widely described as follows: French people eat heavy and fatty foods (including foie gras and rich cheeses), but they don't get fat because they drink red wine. This wonderfully wistful theory remains to be proven, but for me, there is a more salient and intriguing French paradox: While history is woven into almost every aspect of their culture, the French also insist on the fullness of the here and now. The French language has a word for it: *s'attarder*, which means "to draw out," "to linger," "to pause over." Could this be the key to the French art of living well? Expanding time, "being there," taking in all the pleasure that's to be had? Not so much to seize the day as to seize the *moment* and make it last?

As we have seen, language often unwittingly reveals the values of a culture: In English, we "spend" and "invest" time on a project, with implied monetary results. In French, one simply "passes," "devotes," or "consecrates" time. Whereas, in English, people and even objects seem to be in a hurry, politicians "run" for office, and refrigerators and fans also "run," in French, politicians "present themselves" for election (*se présenter*), and machines "walk" (*marcher*). Whereas Americans "run out" of milk, in French, milk is missing (*manquer*). In English, you give someone the "runaround," but in French, you send them on a walk (*envoyer balader*). Your cup may "run over" in the United States, but in France, it overflows (*déborder*).

These examples are simply the tip of the iceberg. There's something profound about linguistic expressions that indicate a rushed sense of time, on the one hand, and a more serene approach, on the other. Anyone who has fought their way through the métro stop at Châtelet at rush hour, however, will probably disagree. Let's just say that the general principle holds.

SMALL PLEASURES

The most time-sensitive modern-day French writer, Philippe Delerm, defines himself as someone who loves the spectacle of life. Described by critics as "an epicurean," "a positive minimalist," and "the inventor of literary instantaneity," Delerm captures and magnifies seemingly insignificant moments. Of the fifty-some books he has published, the most famous remains *La Première Gorgée de bière* (The First Sip of Beer), translated into English as *The Small Pleasures of Life*. In it, he deliciously dissects fleeting moments of bliss. The first sip of beer: "It's the only one that counts." That first sip gives the false sensation of the infinite: fugitive happiness. The froth, the honey color, liquid sunshine.

Delerm invites us to accompany him in other sensory delights. The aroma of apples penetrates the cellar, evoking all things autumn: school, purple ink on paper, rain on windowpanes, long evenings . . . But the smell of apples goes beyond autumn—it conjures up high grasses and dew-covered orchards; the colors red, brown, and green; sweet and acidic tastes; and the painful realization that we no longer have access to the slowness embodied in apples.

I can easily dive into Delerm's text and imagine myself as the first-person narrator—his *I* becomes my *I*, and his *we*, our *we*. It's the end of summer and the telephone rings.

"Would you like to go pick blackberries?"

"I was just going to ask you the same thing!"

The old friend and I soon embark on an outing in the woods. Ebony berries peek through the dull green leaves. Our picking is random and undisciplined. Two or three jars of jam will be enough—or maybe we'll get a few more and make a refreshing sorbet. Some of the berries get eaten along the way, and our hands are now covered with stains of purple juice that we try to wipe away on the grass. We walk along the hilly road between reddening ferns and pearl-covered heather. After a rainstorm, the light is still a bit warm. We have gathered blackberries, we have gathered up the summer. We are now sliding into autumn.

For me, Delerm's most alluring vignette is "We Could Almost Eat Outside." The French love to eat outdoors, as you know from seeing the packed tables in front of cafés, even in the winter, when people are bundled up in scarves and gloves, exhaled breaths steaming. The vignette takes place in March, the sun is out, and it is just beginning to feel warm. The table is set inside, and the *crudités* are ready to be devoured. Then someone pipes up, "We could almost eat outside." Is it too late? We could run outside and clean off the table and propose warm sweaters for our guests. Or we could be resigned to eat inside, where it's warm. After all, the chairs are wet, and the garden hasn't really been cleaned up after the winter. But what's important is the conditional tense: "We could almost . . ." The phrase opens up an invented life of possibility, a modest fantasy. You could say, "We could almost have eaten outside . . . ," but that would make it nostalgic. Instead, regardless of the outcome, there remains a moment of honest hesitation in the realm of the possible. There are days when you could almost.

FRENCH LIFE, THEN AND NOW

When you live in the same neighborhood for most of your life, new memories replace old ones, and the objects that define the neighborhood take on new meanings as your interaction changes with them—a palimpsest with many layers. In our American neighborhood, the park with sandpiles and swings that once entertained our young daughters became a playing field for soccer practice and, later, a grassy spot for picnics and, later still, a meeting place with my college students during the coronavirus pandemic. Each of those memories remains, but the new ones become more vivid as the older ones fade. But if you live in a neighborhood and then return some years later, the objects that defined your life there remain fixed in your memory and are difficult to dislodge, like dried chewing gum on an old wooden desk. And so it is when I return to Les Gobelins, an area named for the great tapestry factory just south of the Latin Quarter, where both my daughters were babies, toddlers, and grade schoolers during sequential stays. The landmarks seem to jump out at me from behind the bushes.

Paris becomes a whole new world when you have a child with you. Prim and proper Parisians become different beings when faced with a baby or a small child—they light up, begin making cooing sounds, or start uninvited conversations. It's a surprising joy to watch and to be a part of. But this time I am alone, happily invisible, as I imagine these spaces as they were with small children in tow.

There's the rue Mouffetard, a tiny market street with its uneven cobblestones (the same stones students hurled at police during the 1968 student and worker revolution). It is overflowing with stands of ripe peaches, colorful vegetables of all sorts, and rabbits hanging from their feet in butchers' stands. Pushing a stroller over the cobblestones is almost impossible, especially while carrying bags of groceries, and on a number of occasions, we had to retrace our steps to find a lost sock or toy. One day, in what I now see was a completely absurd act, I gave my wallet to Lise, two years old, who liked to shake it and hear the different rhythms the coins produced as her stroller lumbered over the cobblestones. When we returned home to the apartment on the rue Broca, the wallet had disappeared, having been tossed out somewhere along the way. By this time, we were at the top of the stairs on the third floor, so after unloading the *filets* (the string shopping bags so prevalent at the time), I gathered Lise and the stroller back into my arms, and the three of us trudged down the stairs to return to the rue Mouffetard. A middle-aged woman with curly brown hair and lively eyes was waiting at the bottom——she had already learned from the all-knowing *gardienne* which floor we lived on.

"I found your wallet," she blurted out in French.

"Oh, thank you, thank you," I replied. "My toddler had been holding it. You're so kind."

"Well, that was a pretty stupid idea, to let her have your wallet, wasn't it? You should never let your toddler hold your wallet," she said, repeating the obvious lesson, as French maternal types are wont to do.

"You're so right," I concurred. "That was a stupid thing to do. You are very nice to have returned the wallet."

"Won't there be a reward?" she ventured.

"Yes, of course. What sort of reward do you mean?"

"Well, whatever you have will be fine."

Never having been confronted with that question, but happy to try to comply, I opened my wallet to find that the only cash in it was a hundred-franc note, the French franc equivalent of twenty-five dollars (and the jingling coins).

"This is all I have," I said while sheepishly but slightly begrudgingly extending the note in her direction. It seemed like quite a bit of money to me. "Unless you'd also like the change."

"No, no," she countered, slipping the bill into her pocket. "That will be fine." She flashed a quick smile in recognition of her good Samaritan act, made a 180-degree turn on one heel, and headed toward the end of the courtyard.

"Thank you again—I really appreciate it," I mustered.

"*De rien*," she replied over her shoulder. "And remember: never, ever give your wallet to your child. Ever!"

And with those words of memorable wisdom, she vanished around the corner at the end of the courtyard.

Over there, at the base of the rue Mouffetard, is the little playground near Saint Médard, where Lise used to build something resembling sandcastles as a toddler. One Easter, she sat on that green park bench with a dapper elderly man who was content to engage in a long, albeit disjointed conversation about whatever she wanted to talk about—in this case, Easter bunnies and chocolate eggs. On different occasions, what seemed like hours were whiled away in that park as Lise reported to work in the sandpile with bucket and scoop, including in the rain, when the sand stuck together even better for architectural purposes. She teamed up with other children for joint constructions as the rain dripped from their rain slickers and the castles turned to mud.

All the children—okay, and some of us adults—loved the *animaux sur ressorts*, animals on springs that are something like a cross between a mechanical bull and a miniature teeter-totter. They come in the form of ducks, horses, dogs, fish, seahorses, and elephants. We wondered why that favorite playground equipment could rarely be found in the States, and we concluded that, with the possibility of fingers or toes getting caught in the springs (unlikely, but possible), a litigious American society must have decided not to provide them at all. American playgrounds have excised the high slides, the merry-go-rounds, the teeter-totters, the tall swings, and basically anything that has any risk or fun associated with it, but in France these delightful spring-loaded animals remain.

As I look at Square Saint Médard today, I remember that it was visited by two other intriguing species: sparrows and pigeons. The pigeons were known for flying all around the park and generously depositing their white detritus on our hair and clothing. It was always a joke to see who would get hit first. Sparrows were much more beloved. "The sparrow man," a rugged man with baggy pants, came every day with a pocketful of bread crumbs, and the sparrows impatiently awaited his arrival. He would stretch his arms out, palms turned upward, and dozens of sparrows would land on his arms and shoulders, walking their way down to his outstretched hands holding the crumbs. Other sparrows would flitter about, hoping to catch falling crumbs in the air. The bird man inevitably amassed an admiring audience of both children and adults, who were drawn to this aviary spectacle if they happened upon the park at just the right time. Today, you can still feed sparrows, but it is illegal to feed pigeons in Paris—to the tune of a 450-euro fine, and the pigeon population has greatly diminished. Sparrows, too, are in short supply. According to the

League for the Protection of Birds, the sparrow population in Paris has been reduced over the past thirty years by 95 percent because of a lack of habitat. There is now a movement to provide nesting opportunities for the sparrows to bring them back.

Near the playground is the yellow mailbox where, before regular email communication, we used to send postcards—remember postcards?—and letters back to the States. As every parent knows, mornings can be hectic, as you're helping children of various ages get ready for school as well as gathering your own affairs for the day's work. One day, with two children in tow, I put a little stack of stamped postcards in the letter box at the bottom of the rue Mouffetard, dropped off Laura in her stroller at day care on the rue Censier, and walked with Lise past the Grand Mosque, through the *roseraie* (rose garden) near the rue Geoffroy Saint Hilaire, and to the École Buffon. When she was safely inside the courtyard of the school, I then took a glorious shortcut across the Jardin des Plantes, which was filled with hydrangea and rhododendrons, en route for the Jussieu station, where the métro would take me to the Bibliothèque Nationale (then, the BN) and my day's work. Arriving at the station, I saw that I no longer had my Carte Orange (a métro pass that has been replaced by the Pass or Carte Navigo) in my bag. "I must have accidentally mailed it with the postcards," I lamented, while retracing my steps. Finally, back to the apartment on the rue Broca, I stuffed some tape in my bag and headed back to the mailbox at the bottom of the rue Mouffetard. I taped a scribbled note to the yellow box in French: "Dear Mail Carrier, I'm afraid I've accidentally mailed my métro pass. Would you be so kind as to contact me at the following telephone number? I will then come to retrieve it. With many thanks to you . . ."

Because my pass was lost, I would have to use métro tickets until it was returned or, if my pass had been mailed to a transatlantic destination, until I bought a new one. I then set out for Jussieu and a long day at the BN. Several days later, when I had given up on hearing from the nice *facteur* (postman) who was to have rescued my métro pass, Laura was experimenting with all the zippers in my book bag (not my wallet this time) and—*voilà!* The missing métro pass reappeared in a never-used pocket of the bag. I considered writing another note to tape to the yellow mailbox: "Dear Mail Carrier, You know the métro pass I thought I had mailed last week? Well, it turns out that . . ." but that seemed a bit excessive.

Just below Saint Médard, look at the now-paved-in area where the musician Christian Bassoul sings and plays his guitar and accordion every Sunday from 11 A.M. till the closing of the market around 1:30 P.M. For at least the past twenty-five years, Bassoul has played the same timeless songs: Édith Piaf, Georges Moustaki, folk songs everyone knows. Sometimes other invited singers join in at the microphone, and all the onlookers are encouraged to participate by singing along. Bassoul furnishes printouts of the lyrics, for those who don't know them, and it doesn't really matter whether you can carry a tune or not. Others dance—polkas, waltzes, swing, invented forms. When quite small, Lise and Laura loved to sing along, sometimes furnishing their own lyrics . . . but as they grew older, that traditional French music seemed hopelessly *vieux jeu* (old-fashioned). Now young adults, they would probably welcome it once again.

And walking southward, looking up, I see the balcony of the apartment we rented at 10 avenue des Gobelins, on the sixth floor. When we first moved in, we began to dry clothes on a rack on the balcony until we learned from our landlady

Françoise that such activity is taboo. *Pas de linge sur le balcon* (No laundry on the balcony). Drying clothes on a balcony makes it look as though you're living in a developing country, explained Françoise, who knew just about everything you would ever want to know and more. It's uncouth and ugly, she told me, and it destroys the neighborhood if people see clothes drying on your balcony. *L'horreur!* Better to jump off the balcony if you have to, but by all means, do not have clothes drying on it. Instead, do what everyone else in Paris does: if the laundry racks don't fit in your bathroom because it's so small that your husband's knees hit the wall while he's on the toilet and he can touch all four walls while he's sitting there, past the shower on one side and past the lavatory on the other, then put them in your living room when the sofa bed isn't open. Right. You can't walk around it while it's there, and you'll be confined to a four-foot-square space, but your laundry will be dry and, most important, the neighbors will be happy.

On the corner of the rue du Fer à Moulin from our apartment is the Brûlerie des Gobelins, a coffee-roasting facility and sales point. With the doors open, the glorious aroma of roasting espresso beans wafted up to our balcony (the one with no clothes on it) every few days.

When we lived on the courtyard side of 10 avenue des Gobelins a few years later, Lise and her neighbor friend Marie, both twelve, set up a pulley-style clothesline from our living room to Marie's bedroom. This was no easy feat. The girls tied a cord to balled-up socks and then hurled the socks across the courtyard to the opposite window. They missed it on the first four attempts, but the fifth one was the charm. They could then attach notes with clothespins and reel them back and forth across the courtyard. A friendly rivalry evolved to see who could send the very first note on the line each morning. How it was that the aesthetically conscious neighbors didn't object to the makeshift clothesline, I cannot recall, but the setup provided hours of creative notes, games, and activities. Today, the same girls would no doubt play video games on their cell phones, but in this case, Lise and Marie were able to reap the harvest of their ingenuity.

Strategically placed on the corner of the rue Poliveau and the rue Geoffroy Saint Hilaire, a makeshift candy shop remained open only during lunchtime and after-school hours. It was on almost every child's way home. Because a daily stop there would likely have been a request from Lise and Laura, we made a deal that they could have *souris* (mice), gummy candies in the shape of mice, but only on Fridays, which we called *vendredi-souris* (Friday mice). What is it about mice in France? The Tooth Fairy is the Petite Souris (the little mouse), and Jean de La Fontaine's famous fable (reworking Aesop) depicts a mouse saving a lion. Could the positive spin on mice have anything to do with the word's homonym? In French, *souris* is both "mouse" and a conjugation of the verb *sourire* (to smile). Of all the choices in the candy shop, both girls always wanted a Friday mouse, and those pinkish-gray delicacies kept them going for the entire year.

Across the way, I can see Nicolas, the ubiquitous wine store with many small outlets throughout Paris. That's where I would pick up a bottle of wine, daughters in tow, on our way to friends' apartments for dinner. Even though we didn't have much room, shortly before we left that neighborhood for the last time, we decided to invite a few friends who had been so welcoming and hospitable to us. Champagne was needed for the occasion, but I was tied up in the kitchen, so I sent Lise and Laura, aged twelve and nine, to Nicolas with enough money to buy two modest bottles.

"Just ask for the sales clerk's recommendations," I told them.

After they left, I thought, *This would be unbelievable in the States, but I think it's doable here, since the clerk will probably recognize them.*

Indeed, after about fifteen minutes they returned with the perfect bottles, already chilled for the evening.

"Did he ask you anything about why you were buying the champagne?" I inquired.

"Oh yes!" they replied in unison. "He wanted to know how many people were coming for dinner and what we were having."

Until 2009, establishments were allowed to serve wine, hard cider, and beer to minors ages sixteen to eighteen, and all alcoholic beverages to those over eighteen. Now French youth are prohibited from drinking any alcohol before eighteen (except when with parents), but based on what I've observed, the law isn't carefully enforced. Many a high school student has stopped by a café for a *panaché* (half lemon soda, half beer) on the way home. A less harsh version of the notion of "forbidden fruit" seems to produce much healthier attitudes toward alcohol in France than in the United States, although, according to the World Health Organization, binge drinking among teenagers has risen across the planet in recent years.

Finally, there's the little restaurant on the rue du Banquier where couscous is served every Friday (the traditional day for couscous in North Africa). Farid always greeted us with an ear-to-ear smile, and we exchanged mini-stories about our respective weeks. He serves Algerian couscous: mouth-watering pieces of chicken falling off the bone, chickpeas, turnips, and carrots

in a clear broth . . . with lots of *harissa* on the side (a spicy con-
diment made from chilis, cumin, garlic, coriander, and caraway
seed). Tunisian couscous is similar to Algerian but often has a
tomato base. Sometimes raisins and toasted almonds are added
to the couscous, but not on the rue du Banquier. This was no-
frills couscous, and it was delicious. In that homey little restaurant, Lise and Laura (along with their friends François and
Matthias) began to develop a taste for strong spices, as they
cautiously added more *harissa* on each visit, to Farid's delight.

Memories of cobblestone streets and pigeons and schoolyards
and a yellow mailbox and a lost-and-found métro pass and new
friends swirl in my head on a brief walk as I remember life with
two young children near the rue Mouffetard. The joy of small,
seemingly insignificant moments so prevalent in French culture
had made their mark on all of us.

STROLLING WITH GHOSTS

Some may find it lugubrious, but I share the passion of many
French citizens for strolling among dead people as they lie
peacefully in their tombs. Père Lachaise, the most illustrious of
French cemeteries, houses the remains of over a million people.
Stars ranging from Chopin to Édith Piaf to Jim Morrison are
now buried there, but the cemetery had a bumpy beginning.

In the early nineteenth century, the graveyards of central
Paris were filled to capacity, so Napoléon ordered the construction of new ones outside Paris's city limits. While Père Lachaise
is beautifully situated on a chiseled hillside, at the time of its
construction, it was considered too far away and not yet "conse-
crated." Virtually no one wanted to be buried there. But a ruse

was devised to attract the public. The remains of two of France's greatest authors, La Fontaine and Molière, would be transferred there—and it worked! The cachet of being buried near these important figures did the trick.

Père Lachaise impresses by its scope and its splendor, but my favorite death walk is in the more modest Montparnasse Cemetery, in the south of Paris. All the tombs have pride of place among the tree-lined paths. Not far from the teeming boulevard du Montparnasse and the avenue du Maine, this oasis of a cemetery is at once reassuring and magical. The names roll by as I stroll among the tombs—burial sites of individuals, families, and collectives such as the Ossuaire des soeurs de Notre Dame de l'assistance maternelle (Ossuary of the Sisters of Our Lady of Maternal Assistance). Statues are perched atop some of the tombs, which I first assumed were commissioned by families in honor of the deceased. Upon closer examination, though, I realized that the statues were made by the sculptors on whose graves they rested. In the early twentieth century, the sculptor Henri Laurens—or whoever survived him—chose a colossal Henry Moore–like sculpture from his own collection for his tomb. A massive nude figure sits with its feet more or less in Fish pose, if you know yoga, and its head almost buried in the torso, depicting mourning, *la douleur* (in this case, "grief"). Is it a self-portrait in sculpture? But, no. As I walk around the back, I see that the figure's hips are round, suggesting femininity, and a closer look reveals breasts pressed against the stomach by the bowed head. (I personally can't contort myself in quite that way, but the statue looks convincing.) It turns out that Marthe Laurens, the sculptor's wife, was also his model. I circle the statue several times, marveling at its solemnity and its sweeping curves. Just down the lane, another statue portrays a shepherd crouched over his staff, as if in prayer, or to rest, or maybe to mourn. This one was also sculpted by the inhabitant of the tomb, Baltasar Lobo, who, as I later learned, was known for his ebullient sculptures of mothers and children and bodies in movement. Lobo's other statues will continue to evoke motion and life, but this shepherd seems to imply *You have done your work. Rest well.*

So many souls have lived on in the decaying or desiccated remains lying under these beautiful monuments. Many of the recent tombs are showier, more *bling, bling* (which the French maintain is a French expression), and formal flower arrangements covered with cellophane are sometimes piled above them. But, for me, the beauty lies in the original simplicity of this unassuming cemetery. On the tomb of the writers and activists Jean-Paul Sartre and Simone de Beauvoir, a wildflower has been placed, its stem held down by a smooth stone. It was probably put there by an admirer this very morning. And the notes of acolytes, written in several languages, have been placed on the tomb, weighted under stones: One, written on a métro ticket, says in Italian, "*Filosofia = Vita*" (Philosophy = Life). Another reads "Thank you" in Greek. There is also a note, "Simone, The First Sex," written in English, meant undoubtedly to herald Beauvoir's groundbreaking book *The Second Sex*, but also to set the record straight. For an added bit of splash, the tombstone is covered with lipstick kisses.

Not far away, near the western end of the cemetery, is the sepulcher of Baudelaire, a nondescript tomb. Today, a blue paper flower, intricately formed, lies on the concrete slab. On it, lines from Baudelaire's sonnets are inscribed in beautiful French script. I can make out only a few words at a time because the petals fold at various angles.

The effect is much like that of refrigerator poems made with Magnetic Poetry: *Ô vierges / l'écume / A la pale / tempête / impregnés / caresses* (O virgins / the foam / In the pale / storm / filled with / caresses). It took an internet search to figure out which poems had been carefully penned on the petals and—eureka! I found Baudelaire's poems on lesbian desire—*les femmes damnées* (condemned women)—poems that were banned after their publication in 1857. Determined and resilient, these words come alive on the petals of a blue flower—at least for today. And one of Ronsard's most beautiful sonnets pops into my mind; it evokes death, but also the cycles of life and death. Above the decaying body, flowers grow.

Pour obsèques reçois mes larmes et mes pleurs,
Ce vase plein de lait, ce panier plein de fleurs,
Afin que vif et mort, ton corps ne soit que roses.

(As a funeral offering, please accept my tears and my cries,
This vase filled with milk, this basket filled with flowers,
So that in death, as in life, your body will be nothing but
    roses.)

As I prepare to reenter the commotion of the boulevard du Montparnasse via the rue Huyghens, I glance behind me across the resting tombstones and the tranquil, verdant walkways. I realize that the most fascinating tombs in the Montparnasse Cemetery have lives of their own, as did the people represented and remembered here. These evolving tombs bear witness to the joy of having lived.

TAKING IT SLOW

In 2021, the nationalized French train company reinstituted the overnight train from Paris to several southern cities. Paris-Nice leaves at 11 p.m. and arrives in Marseille at 6 a.m. and Nice at 9 a.m., which leaves at 10 P.M. and arrives at nine o'clock the next morning. Ten other night trains throughout France are expected to be added before 2030. An active lobbying group, Oui au train de nuit! (Yes to the Night Train), celebrated the first of what it hopes will be many victories. Its aims are ecological—to reduce fuel-consuming air travel—but the group is also issuing a plea to slow down. A permanent sign on the window of each train car reads: LAISSEZ-VOUS RÊVER (Let Yourself Dream), reminiscent of the French saying *"Rêver sa vie pour vivre son rêve"* (Dream your life to live your dream). Even the high-speed train company in France is urging us to take it easy.

French employment policies regarding working time and vacation days speak to the vital importance of time (off) in French society. The full-time workweek in France is thirty-five hours. A minimum of twenty-five paid vacation days during (not after) the first year of employment is mandated by the government, time off that extends upward with seniority to over nine weeks in some French companies. As a means of comparison, the United States is one of the few countries in the world to have no government mandates about minimum paid leave. How can the policies of two global, northern, industrialized countries differ so starkly from each other? Something about chickens and eggs: Are the French governmental and social policies in favor of a less frantic and more leisurely lifestyle the result of a culture that refuses to be dominated by work, or do the people promote these values, and they then become policy? Or both?

The television channel France 2 recently reported on an Algerian immigrant, Salim, who had lived in France for thirteen years, earned a master's degree in physics, was married, and had a French child. He had worked fifty-seven hours a week with several part-time salaries (all legal and all taxed), but his naturalization request was denied on the grounds that he had worked too many hours. The newscaster jokingly reported that Salim worked too much to be truly French. But when journalists questioned the relevant authorities, they learned that Salim had indeed broken the Code du travail by working more than forty-eight hours per week, the legal maximum ("meant to protect workers' health"). When the media focused their attention on the case, the Ministry of Citizenship retracted its negative decision and approved Salim's naturalization. As absurd as it seems, the joke was true: At least upon a first attempt, Salim could not be considered French because he didn't take enough time off.

Last summer, despite having lived for years in France, I had an abrupt awakening as to my own tendency to let an American sense of time and work creep in. Our friends Thomas and Nacho were in the process of moving from one apartment to another and needed to vacate their current flat by 10:30 A.M. on the dot, when the rental agent would be coming by to do the *état des lieux* (final check). Thomas determined that we could carry all the myriad stacked boxes and load them into the truck in about an hour. So, we arrived at 9 A.M. to make sure that there was a little leeway. Thomas had just prepared a French press *café* and asked if we would like coffee and croissants.

"Hadn't we better get started carrying things down?" I inquired, in my most American of ways, as I looked at the tall piles of boxes.

My husband, Mark, helpfully added, "We're ready to roll."

But in France, morning is morning, and coffee is coffee, so Thomas filled our espresso cups with dark magic and said that the others would be figuring out how to load the truck, so we should just take it easy for a moment.

But we hadn't even started!

As I sipped my espresso, I realized that the clock was ticking, and as far as I could tell, the boxes stacked to the ceiling would take more than an hour to load. Thomas was relaxed, though, assured that it would all work out one way or another.

We then decided to form an assembly line from the second floor to the truck: Thomas would take each box, go halfway down the stairs, and hand it to Mark, who would carry the box down to me on the ground floor, where I would take the box outside to Nacho, Thomas's husband, who would then hand it off to Pablo, who was packing the truck.

We had had our coffee, but as soon as it was finished, Thomas told us that we should have croissants. Meanwhile, the coffee maker needed to be washed and packed away, which I did when we had a lull between large items as Pablo loaded them carefully into the truck.

Why weren't all these dishes packed away earlier? I wondered as I washed the cups and coffee maker and tried to find something to dry them with. (Of course, all the dish towels had long since been taken out.)

The answer was, obviously, *You don't just skip coffee and conviviality because you're moving, silly American.*

We continued the assembly line, moving more and more quickly, all of us sweating like elite athletes. It was now 10:20, and the elegant blonde agent had arrived early and was leaning against the wall in the hallway, arms folded, visibly waiting. Just a few last touches, a final lamp to load, and then the truck had to be moved from the loading zone.

Stuffing a bag of now-smashed croissants into my hand, Thomas said, "I guess we won't have time to eat these this morning—enjoy!"

I protested, saying that he and Nacho should take them for the road, but he replied, "No, that's the least we can do."

Because they needed to get the truck out of the loading zone without delay, I reluctantly accepted the flattened croissants, and off we all went, into the rest of our day. The croissants were delicious but, above all, we had had our coffee.

Un dernier mot (A last word)

L'heure de la fin des découvertes ne sonne jamais.
(The bell sounding the end of discoveries will never ring.)

—Colette

As I look out the window above the boulevard du Montparnasse, I see mother-of-pearl clouds floating like rabbits with floppy ears across the sky. *Pareidolia*, I think to myself, having learned that cool word just last year—"the tendency of humans to assign meaning to random shapes." It strikes me that we all engage in a bit of pareidolia as we look at another culture. If we can't make sense of it, we fill in the blanks in our own way.

I realize that my vision of France has a touch of pareidolia with more than a pinch of idealization and romanticism, cut by a modicum of reproach. (If you have ever stood in a long line in France and been surrounded by many gargling sighs of disdain, you know exactly what I mean.)

I've never counted the number of times I've gone to France for visits or longer stays, but each time I leave, I am moved as I walk through the spaces I inhabited at ages nineteen, twenty-seven, thirty-five, and beyond. The association of places and events, like superimposed layers of a medieval manuscript, remains firm. The

Pont Saint Michel, where a young Swedish man, Stefan, stood me up (*m'a posé un lapin*, literally, "left a rabbit for me," speaking of rabbits); the copy of the Statue of Liberty I climbed in the Jardin du Luxembourg, only to be reprimanded and ordered down by an angry police officer; the bistro where my favorite professor took me to dinner when I was a graduate student; the Saint Médard Square, where my daughters played in the sandbox as toddlers, wearing their miniature overalls—each spot holds a sense of wonder, of finitude, but also of continuity and renewal. The Pont Saint Michel is now dotted with couples (lovers who showed up!). After being absent for a few years for refurbishing, the Statue of Liberty is back hoisting her lamp high in the Jardin du Luxembourg. Young Americans flock there to see the model of their famous landmark, though none I have seen has been daring or idiotic enough to climb it. Professors and students are having lunch together in cafés all over the city, and toddlers wearing miniature overalls are still shoveling sand into their blue plastic buckets. Years from now, they will walk by these same places and evoke their own reconstructions of the past, mixed with the present. Meanwhile, I am here, recollecting, imagining, and projecting these places into the future.

"No matter how long a log stays in the river," the African proverb goes, "it still won't become a crocodile." When I first heard this saying, I was struck by its determinism—it seemed to claim that no one can change from an assigned role. But I've come to see it in a different way. I now imagine that African log on the Niger River, sensing what it's like to float and to glide through the currents. Maybe some of the DNA of the crocodiles swimming next to it has rubbed off on it. And maybe, sometimes, the log is even mistaken for a crocodile. And although the log may leave the river, it will always bear traces of having lived in that habitat.

I am like that log. Even after living in France for about ten years now, I will never become French, as I had long ago fervently hoped to. But something else happened along the way. Many of my life's discoveries—especially about the sumptuousness of being here, now—have come from living in France. Like many Americans before and after me, I will carry the imprint of quirky and often loveable people, of stunning physical landscapes, of invigorating debates, of—how else to put it?—joie de vivre.

The floppy brown hat I wore during my first days in Paris, now covered with dust, hangs over the back of my closet shelf like one of Dalí's melting clocks, conjuring that awkward nineteen-year-old girl of the past who has and has not disappeared. It also suggests the timelessness of travel and of being otherwise, elsewhere.

For me, French culture is not necessarily the height of civilization (depending on how that is defined); nor does it represent "the best of all possible worlds," as Candide ironically intones. But the infusion of other peoples into this already culturally rich society has made it richer, and better equipped to think differently. Whether it's over coq au vin or couscous, to the backbeat of Bizet or African drums, through the eyes of an aging farmer from Auvergne or a young Parisian professional—the French are still inventing new ways of living well. Each time I return to France, I discover, rediscover, and discover again.

"We'll always have Paris," Humphrey Bogart's Rick famously utters; and we'll always have *Casablanca*. But in that oft-quoted line, Bogart's character is simply rephrasing Seneca: "What you have you can lose, but what you have had, you keep forever." All of us fortunate enough to have at least dabbled in the French joie de vivre can keep it—in our lives, in our imaginations, or in our dreams.

Photo Permissions

62   *Carte du Tendre* (1654), courtesy of the Bibliothèque nationale de France

86   Bibliothèque nationale, Richelieu site, courtesy of AP/ Michel Euler

102   Fresnel lens, photograph © Mark S. McNeil

118   Léon-Ernest Drivier, *La Joie de vivre* (*The Joy of Living*, 1937), courtesy of EUtouring.com

119   Aristide Maillol, *La Douleur* (*Sorrow*, 1922), © Mark S. McNeil

122   Camille Claudel, *Vertumne et Pomone* (1905), Musée Rodin, Paris, courtesy of Vanni Archive/Art Resource, New York

123   Jean-Baptiste Greuze, *La Dévideuse de laine* (*The Wool Winder*, 1759), courtesy of the Frick Collection

124   Édouard Manet, *Le Déjeuner sur l'herbe* (*The Luncheon on the Grass*, 1863), Musée d'Orsay, courtesy of Vanni Archive/Art Resource, New York

196   Flower in the Montparnasse Cemetery, author's photograph

Acknowledgments

I am grateful to the following publishers for permission to quote from these works: Éditions Gallimard for *La Première Gorgée de bière et autres plaisirs minuscules* by Philippe Delerm; Éditions du Minuit and Pantheon for *L'Amant* by Marguerite Duras; Warner Chappell Music and Hal Leonard LLC for "Des laids des laids" by Serge Gainsbourg; Paramount Global for the dialogue from *Emily in Paris;* and Éditions du Seuil for *La Tour Eiffel* by Roland Barthes.

My deepest thanks extend to Charles Spicer for his astute and generous role as editor, and to Stephen Power, formerly of St. Martin's Press, who first proposed the idea of writing a book based on a course I taught. Gifted readers whose ideas are reflected here (and whose thoughtfulness will not be forgotten) include Maëva Bekkar, Eric Gutierrez, Susan Jaret McKinstry, Elisabeth Yandell McNeil, Laura Yandell McNeil, Mark McNeil, Marie Ménard, and Thomas Roman. I also owe a continuing debt of gratitude to my colleague-friends Sarah Anthony, Scott Carpenter, Stephanie Cox, Chérif Keïta, Christine

Lac, Éva Pósfay, Sandra Rousseau, Cynthia Shearer, and Dana Strand; to my students, who teach me as I teach them; and to Carleton College. For many reasons, the book would not have been possible without the additional contributions of Gwenda and Imad Wehbe (*sine quibus non*), Malcolm Bell, Jean-Louis Besse, Thomas Clough, Heather Dubrow, Dianne Dunn, Eve Frédérix, Yasmina Berchiche Galtier, Mary Lewis Grow, Juliette Frédérix Joly, Chantal Le Brun, Élisabeth Le Brun, Elizabeth McKinsey, Nacho Ormaechea, Malika Ouchoutta, Josette Rolinat, Eve Rosenblat, Maïmouna Touré-Keïta, Carol Yandell Williams, Mark Williams, and all the Wehbes. I warmly dedicate this book to my inimitable families—Yandell-McNeil-Lukk, Williams, Wade, Jaret-McKinstry, and Habig, who embody *la joie de vivre* at every turn.

Index

L'Académie française, 173
adulthood, age of, in France, 170–71
Africa, artwork of, return of, 162
alcohol, 1–3, 192
Algeria, 161
    War of Independe-nce, 160–61
Amboise, Leonardo's studio in, 115
Americans
    being identified as, 5–6, 176
    French opinions about, 141, 169
amuse-bouche, 11
apartments, small, 18, 190
apéritif, 2
April Fool's Day, 71–72
Arabe du coin (the Arab on the corner), 153
art
    classes in schools, 170
    in Paris, 110–40
    state support of, 115
arts urbain (murals), 125–31
astronauts, 17–18
Atelier des Lumières, 106–9
Aubenas, Florence, 99
avenue des Gobelins, 190

baguette, 25–26
bakery, small-town, 149–51
banlieue (suburbs), 152

Bassoul, Christian, 189
baths, Gallo-Roman, 34
Baudelaire, Charles, 90–93, 114, 195–96
Beauvoir, Simone de, 104, 195
Belgians
    humor of, 70–71
    joke about, 71
Bergson, Henri, 70
Bianco, Renato (René Bianchi), 27
Bible, French translation of, 172
Bibliothèque François Mitterrand,
    89–90
Bibliothèque nationale de France, 85–89,
    188
birds, feeding them, 187–88
bise, faire le (kissing), 31–32
Bonjour (greeting), 146–47
books, 82–90, 105–6
bookshops, 81–82
Bourdier, Nicolas, 151
Bourdieu, Pierre, 78
breakfast, 147–48
Brulé, Gaël, 32
Buathier, Lucie, 136–37
bûche de Noël, 15

C215, 126
Cabrel, Francis, 139–40

Camus, Albert, *The Stranger,* 84
Carter, Jimmy, 65
Casey, 142
Catherine de Médicis, 27–28, 61, 148–49
cats, Baudelaire's, 92–93
celebrations
    food at, 12–16
    music at, 137
    wine at, 191–92
cemeteries, 193–97
Centre de danse du Marais, 56
Champs Élysées, 47
Charles IX, 148–49
Château Gontier, 152
chefs, competition of, 25
chevreuil (venison), 14
children, having and caring for them in
    Paris, 184–93
Choderlos de Laclos, Pierre, (*Dangerous
    Liaisons*), 103–4
Christmas dinner, 13–16
City of Light, 103
Claudel, Camille, 121
    Vertumne et Pomone, 121, *122*
Cléo from 5 to 7, 132–33
clothing, fur in, 5
clubs, for dancing, 56
Code du travail (Labor Code), 16, 198
coffee, 57
Comédie Française, 142
comics, stand-up, 73–75
Compagnon, Antoine, 9
conversation, topics and styles of, 159–60,
    163
cookbooks, 22
cooking, 18–23, 26
cooking show, 26
coronovirus pandemic, 98
couscous, 24
Covid-19, 98, 115, 149
    lockdowns, 69
croissant, 25
cuisine, French, foreign dishes in, 24–26
Cuisine ouverte cooking show, 26
Curie, Marie, 155
Cyrano de Bergerac (fictional), 155–57

daisy petals, plucking, 68
Dalí, Salvador, 107–9

dance, 55–56
    clubs, 56
deaths, certification of, 148
debating style of conversation, 159–60,
    163
de Gaulle, Charles, 155
Delacroix, Eugène, 123
Delerm, Philippe, 182–84
délicieux, 20
Descartes, 76–77
dictée (dictation exercise in schools), 165
dictionaries, 9
Diderot, Denis, 104
    Encyclopédie, 105–6
dining, 11–18
    unspoken rules of, 23–24
doctors, small-town, 148–49
Doisneau, Robert, 163
doux (sweet), 33
Draï, Joséphine, 67
drinking, 94–95
drinks, 12
Drivier, Léon-Ernest, *La Joie de vivre,*
    116–17, *118*
drying clothes, 189–90
du Bellay, Joachim, 172–73
Ducasse, Alain, 17
Duhamel, Georges, 136
Duras, Marguerite, *L'Amant (The Lover),*
    96–98

École élémentaire Buffon, 163–68
edibles, French, 5
Edict of Villers-Cotterêts, 172
education
    French and American, compared,
        170
    See also schools
Eiffel, Gustave, 110–11
Eiffel Tower, 110–12
    lighting of, at sunset, 112
Emily in Paris (Netflix series), 82–83
English language, heard by French
    speakers, 49
Enlightenment, Age of, 103–6
entrée (appetizer), 11
l'épectase (dying during orgasm), 64
Erasmus Rural, 151
exercise parks and stations, 51–55

Fairey, Shepard, 126
fairy tales, French, 73
famille (family), 143–48
farming, 151–52
Fary (comic), 73–74
Faure, Félix, 64
Fête de la musique, 138
films, 131–36
    humor in, 133–36
Finkielkraut, Alain, 142
flâneur, 114
Flaubert, Gustave, 9
    Madame Bovary, 83
Flemings, 71
flowers, 23–24, 28–29
flower shops, 29–31
Fontainebleau, 33
food
    not allowed at work, 16
    See also cooking; dining
food and dining, French paradox, 181
fountains, 33–34
France
    L'Hexagone nickname, 45
    ranked first in pleasure, worldwide,
        32–33
France Culture (radio station), 60
François I, 115, 172
Franklin, Benjamin, 179
French language, 5–6, 171–79
    bodily words describing learning, 77
    heard by English speakers, 49
    history of, 172
    idiomatic expressions based on food,
        20–21
    learning it, 2, 173–79
    mistakes and pitfalls, 174–75
    swear words, 164, 177
    vocabulary, 173, 175, 178, 179, 181–82
French paradox (diet), 181
French people
    differences from Americans, 179,
        181–82, 199–200
    epitomes who define, 155, 159
    individualism of, 141–42
    looking French, 3–4, 8
    new, combination of natives and
        immigrants, 45–46
    stereotypes about, 8–9

"Frère Jacques" (song), 2
Fresnel, Augustin-Jean, 101
friends, making, 169–70
fur, in clothing, 5

Gainsbourg, Serge, "Des laids des laids,"
    158
Gallo-Roman period, 34
gays, 58
gendered stereotypes of sexual prowess, 58
Gilets jaunes ("Yellow Vests"), 163
Giono, Jean, 149
Godard, Jean-Luc, *Breathless,* 153
grande culture, 142
Grands Moulins area, 126
Grasse (perfume capital of the world),
    28–29
Greuze, Jean-Baptiste, 121–22
    La dévideuse de laine, 123
Griveaux, Benjamin, 65–66
Guignol puppet theater, 72–73
Guitel, Olivier, 69

Hamel family (hosts), 4, 6
hammam (Turkish bath), 41–44
handball (French style), 48–50
Hanrot, Zita, 67
Haussmann, Georges-Eugène, 101–2
Henri II, 61–64
history, as taught in schools, 160
honorifics (Madame, etc.), 146
host families, 4–6, 19, 143–48
Hugo, Victor
    Quasimodo character, 158
    The Hunchback of Notre Dame, 84
humor, 69–75

immigrants, music of, 136–37
industrial buildings, repurposed as art
    repositories, 106
intellectuals, 78–81
Intra Larue, 127–28
Invader, 128
Ionesco, Eugène, *L'Avenir est dans
    les oeufs (The Future Is in Eggs),* 152

Jacob, Irène, 99
Jardin du Luxembourg, 202
jaywalking, 73–74

jazz, 136
"Je l'aime à mourir," 139–40
J'EXISTE, 127
joie de vivre (French art of living well),
   9–10, 203
Jollien, Alexandre, *L'Éloge de la faiblesse,*
   157

Klimt, Gustav, 106–7
Kundera, Milan, 48

La Chapelle-en-Juger, 150–51
La Fontaine, Jean, 194
   Fables of, 158
Lang, Jack, 137
language learning, by immersion, 2
La Pléiade, 173
Latin Quarter, 4
Laurens, Henri, 194
Laurent (street artist), 127
lecture sous les arbres (reading under the
   trees activity), 98–100
Le Dîner des cons (film), 134–35
Le Havre, 3
le moins pire, 7
Le Monde, sex column in, 60
Leonardo da Vinci, 115
   Mona Lisa, 114
Les Gobelins neighborhood, 184–93
Les Halles, 126
Les Visiteurs (film), 133–34
LGBTQ+ interest, 127
libraries, 85–90
Lido de Paris, 5
light, 100–109
lighthouses, 101
literature, 155–59
living well. *See* joie de vivre
Lobo, Baltasar, 195
"Loi Taubira" on slavery, 160
Louis, Édouard, 99
Louis XIV, loves of, 64
Lumière, Louis, 131
lunchtime, 16–17
Lycée Montaigne, 168–69

Mabanckou, Alain, 153
Macron, Emmanuel, 20, 160–61
Magnol, Marcel, 149

Maïa Mazaurette (sex columnist), 60–61
Maillol, Aristide, *La Douleur (Pain),*
   117–19, *119*
Manet, Édouard, *Le Déjeuner sur l'herbe
   (Luncheon on the Grass),* 123–25,
   124
Marguerite de Navarre, 34
Marie-Antoinette, 25
markets, outdoor, 18–19
Marko 93, 128–31
Marseille, 197
Matisse, Henri, *Le Bonheur de vivre (Joy of
   Life),* 125–26
Maxim's, 5
métro pass, 188–89
Metropolitan Museum of Art, tourists
   in, 113
mind/body question (Descartes), 76–77
minors, buying wine and alcoholic drinks
   by, French law, 192
Miss Tic, 127
Mittelholzer, Anna, 55–56
Mitterand, François, 64–65
Molière, 194
   Tartuffe, 158
Montaigne, Michel de, *Essais,* 93–96
Montalembert, Thibault de, 99
Montmartre, 127
Montparnasse Cemetery, 194–97
mosque, 44
MoSuke restaurant, 26–27
movies. *See* films
M'seddi, Mahmoud, 25–26
murals (street art), 125–31
Musée Rodin, 120–21
music, 136–40
musicians, street, 189
Muslims, 41–44

namedropping, 78
Napoleon III, 102
NDiaye, Marie, 158
neighborhoods, 184–93
New Mexico, 2
New Wave, 132
Nice, 197
Nietzsche, Friedrich, 157–58
night life, 5
North African cuisine, 24, 192–93